"In the Mennonite church, we have si͟x look for in persons whom we call to pastoral ministry. from personal experience and research and analysis from a broad spectrum of church leaders, this brilliant, accessible book gives us eight core competencies (characteristics) of faithful congregations. This book is a must-read for church leaders looking to reawaken a passion for sharing the gospel in our time."

—DOUG KLASSEN, executive minister of Mennonite Church Canada

"In *Reawakened*, Glen Guyton translates the mission of the early church to relevant and practical tools for post-2020 communities of discipleship. This is not a reworking of traditional practices; this is innovation using technology, culture, and change as partners—not barriers—in congregational development. Guyton uses his unique leadership, biblical models, and contemporary trends to form contextual strategies for churches and institutions connected to Christ and community. *Reawakened* is essential resourcing for leaders who understand both the call and the power of the church and are ready to help it reemerge strongly."

—SHANNON DYCUS, dean of students at Eastern Mennonite University

"*Reawakened* is a call for churches everywhere to not just wake up, but adjust the lens of leadership. We are reminded that we don't need another coffee hour or fancy lighting. *Reawakened*, however, compels us to focus on the community, intentional partnerships, and authentic outreach. The eight keys that Glen offers are priceless. Thank you, Glen Guyton, for the wake-up call!"

—LISA JENKINS, lead pastor of St. Matthew's Baptist Church of Harlem

"*Reawakened* not only calls for leaders to understand and cultivate the identity of their faith-based organizations, but carefully outlines the direct path to action for congregational transformation today. Glen Guyton closely examines generational needs, listens attentively, and then creates a detailed path for activating Christ's teachings within the body of the church. Both conversational and practical, this book offers a much-needed guide to reenergize congregations for the complex mission field that is modern society."

—**JANE WOOD**, president of Bluffton University

re*awaken*ed

re*awaken*ed

Activate Your Congregation to *Spark* Lasting Change

Glen Guyton

HERALD
P R E S S

Harrisonburg, Virginia

Herald Press
PO Box 866, Harrisonburg, Virginia 22803
www.HeraldPress.com

Library of Congress Cataloging-in-Publication Data
Names: Guyton, Glen Alexander, 1969- author.
Title: Reawakened : activate your congregation to spark lasting change /
    Glen Alexander Guyton.
Description: Harrisonburg, Virginia : Herald Press, 2021. | Includes
    bibliographical references.
Identifiers: LCCN 2021002299 (print) | LCCN 2021002300 (ebook) |
    ISBN 9781513807638 (hardcover) | ISBN 9781513808079 (paperback) |
    ISBN 9781513807645 (ebook)
Subjects: LCSH: Church. | Theology, Doctrinal.
Classification: LCC BV600.3 .G89 2021 (print) | LCC BV600.3 (ebook) |
    DDC 250—dc23
LC record available at https://lccn.loc.gov/2021002299
LC ebook record available at https://lccn.loc.gov/2021002300

REAWAKENED
© 2021 by Herald Press, Harrisonburg, Virginia 22803. 800-245-7894.
    All rights reserved.
Library of Congress Control Number: 2021002299
International Standard Book Number: 978-1-5138-0807-9
Printed in United States of America
Cover and interior design by Merrill Miller

25 24 23 22 21   10 9 8 7 6 5 4 3 2 1

To God's peace, may we all receive it.
To my family (Cyndi, Andre-A, and Alex),
ministry starts at home.
It has been an honor to serve you.

CONTENTS

FOREWORD

ONE OF THE essential lessons I've learned from over twenty years of studying the church in North America is just how important local context has become. When I first started my graduate studies and research, I honed in on a key tenet: If you could pick your church up, move it to another part of your city or town, and basically keep going without missing a beat, then you're primed for failure. In other words, even as the world was moving toward being more connected and dispersed than ever, the local, the physical, the neighborhood, was rising in prominence.

The 2000s have generally borne this claim out, but with one major caveat. Our local context now extends beyond the physical to the social. If I were to amend my earlier claim to reflect the reality of the modern world, it would change to say: If, tomorrow, your church were suddenly filled with all new people and you could keep going without missing a beat, then you're primed for failure.

The position of the Christian church in America in 2021 is a direct result of failing to grasp this fundamental truth: people and places matter. And this is where Reawakened comes in. This book is a call to return to the fundamentals of people and place, but in a modern context.

The timing for this book couldn't be more important. For too long the church has focused, almost singularly, on itself. In order to reclaim a position of prominence and relevance in the lives of the people the church and its leaders so dearly wish to serve, the lessons of Reawakened must be implemented—and quickly!

What makes the approach outlined in the following pages so compelling is the way Glen Guyton integrates modern research with practical experience to produce insights that are both timeless and incredibly relevant to doing ministry in the twenty-first century. The eight characteristics outlined in the chapters of Reawakened serve as a blueprint for creating a church that could neither be picked up and moved across town or inhabited by all new people without missing a beat. In short, it's a guide for creating relevant congregations and ministries that are intimately connected to the people and places they serve.

My own work has recently led to leading Springtide Research Institute, where we focus on the religious and daily lives of thirteen- to twenty-five-year-olds. In the past year, we've collected over ten thousand surveys and more than 150 interviews with young people on a range of issues. Our data confirm that the trends Glen notes in his book show no sign of slowing down in the coming generations. Young people, more than any other generation, view the church as more disconnected and less trustworthy. The eight characteristics noted in Reawakened can help turn these trends around for the Christian church. This book needs to be taken seriously by those who are truly interested in a flourishing church for generations to come.

My hope for those reading this text is that they come to understand the importance of retaining the values, core beliefs, and lessons that make religion such a vital component of life while also understanding where there is room for innovation. Indeed, to see this modern era as simply another chapter in the long story of innovation that is at the heart of religion in the United States. Reawakened offers a guide for helping visionaries see themselves, in a very practical way, as leaders in this movement.

—*Josh Packard, PhD*
Author of Church Refugees and executive
director of Springtide Research Institute

Introduction

Awake, O sleeper,
rise up from the dead,
and Christ will give you light.
—EPHESIANS 5:14 (NLT)

WHEN I REFLECT on the state of the Christian church in the United States, I can't help but think about the scene from the movie *Monty Python and the Holy Grail*. (For my readers who are younger than Gen X, check it out on YouTube and thank me later.) In the "Bring out your dead" scene, a dirty undertaker and his hirelings pick up the bodies of poverty-stricken people who have died from the plague. The undertaker and his crew of workers throw body after body into a wooden cart. The pile of mud-covered bodies gets higher and higher as the undertaker repeatedly yells, "Bring out your dead," in a monotonous, macabre, joyless, military-like jody. At one stop, an impoverished old man cries out, "I'm not dead yet." The undertaker's helper replies, "Well, you need to go anyway. You'll be dead soon." Back and forth they banter in their dry British humor.

The man is clinging to life but continues to protest his addition to the cart. Eventually, the undertaker clubs the man on the head, knocking him unconscious, and his hirelings throw him onto the cart with the other bodies.

The Monty Python sketch, oddly enough, reminds me of the church. At times I see the church surrounded by hopelessness and death, but not able to make a difference. All around, there is need. People are in trouble, crying for help, but the church in the United States is not standing out as a beacon of hope. The church is calling out for people to join us, crying out to be noticed. To those in the younger generation, the church is insisting, "Hey, I am still here," but this modern world seems to be moving on.

The challenge church leaders face today is that our culture is becoming increasingly skeptical of religious leaders and institutions, leaving churches increasingly marginalized and isolated from the center of community life. Not only is there significant skepticism about churches, but in some circles, there is growing hostility and resentment toward the church because of widely publicized cases of sexual abuse, greed, and partisan politics. Instead of being seen as contributors to the community, churches are increasingly seen as a drain on the community.

A young sociologist friend of mine who studies the decline in church attendance says that more and more people are moving away from the church not because they lack faith in God, but because the church is no longer relevant to meeting their needs. In their book, *Church Refugees*, sociologists Josh Packard and Ashleigh Hope address this idea that the church in the United States has become increasingly irrelevant. They write, "The two most important macro-level trends are undoubtedly the loss of trust in social institutions in general and religious leaders in particular, and the perception that religious institutions are no longer tied into the daily life of individuals as intimately as they once were."[1]

The increasing marginalization of the church in the United States can be seen in dropping levels of church participation. According to a study done by the Pew Research Center, rates of both religious affiliation and religious attendance are declining. "Over the last decade, the share of Americans who say they attend religious services at least once or twice a month dropped by seven percentage points, while the share who say they attend religious services less often (if at all) has risen by the same degree." Today, 54 percent of Americans now say they attend religious services only a few times a year. Only 45 percent of Americans say they visit religious services monthly.[2]

One of the most striking things about the decline in church participation is the generational differences. Participation in the church isn't just decreasing overall—it's decreasing most in the youngest generations. With each new generation, there has been a greater decline in Americans who identify as Christian. Only 49 percent of millennials consider themselves Christian, while among Generation X, one of the smaller generations, with 65 million members, 67 percent identify as Christian. Millennials are the second-largest generation in the U.S. population, with 72 million members, and many of them dropped the habit of participating in church after they graduated high school. The largest generation on the horizon is Gen Z, at 90 million strong. It is not too late for us to adapt and reach them.

Michael O. Emerson and Christian Smith note in their book about evangelicals and race in America that "the organization of American religion is characterized by disestablishment, pluralism, competition, and consumer choice."[3] These factors have contributed to a culture in which many people increasingly choose not to participate in church at all. The church in the United States has become a victim of its own consumerism.

Figure 1. **Large generation gap in American religion**

In 2018/2019, % of U.S. adults who identify as…

	Christian	Non-Christian faiths	Unaffiliated
Silent generation (born 1928–45)	84%	4%	10%
Baby boomers (1946–64)	76	6	17
Generation X (1965–80)	67	6	25
Millennials (1981–96)	49	9	40

In 2018/2019, % of U.S. adults who say they attend religious services…

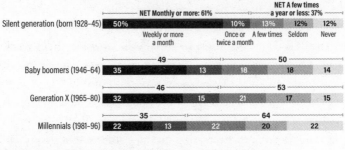

	NET Monthly or more: 61%		NET A few times a year or less: 37%		
	Weekly or more a month	Once or twice a month	A few times a month	Seldom	Never
Silent generation (born 1928–45)	50%	10%	13%	12%	12%
Baby boomers (1946–64)	35	13	18	18	14
Generation X (1965–80)	32	15	21	17	15
Millennials (1981–96)	22	13	22	20	22

Note: Don't know/refused not shown. Generation designations vary by study and source.
Source: Aggregated Pew Research Center political surveys conducted January 2018–July 2019 on the telephone. "In U.S., Decline of Christianity Continues at Rapid Pace," Pew Research Center, October 17, 2019, https://www.pewforum.org/2019/10/17/in-u-s-decline-of-christianity-continues-at-rapid-pace/.

It is no wonder that so many of our churches are increasingly disconnected from the life of their communities and are faced with waning attendance and decreasing financial support. Too many leaders are building empires rather than building up the lives of people.

Some have attempted to respond to these cultural shifts by embracing a form of neo-traditionalism. That is not what this book is advocating. In my experience, "neo" movements are a red herring in the search for a culturally relevant model of church. Neo-traditionalist churches look to the "good old days" as their ideal, and are usually homogenous, rather than modeling the diverse and inclusive nature of the church in the book of Acts. They romanticize a bygone era before technology, the Internet, the dissolution of the nuclear family, and in many cases, before the new, more inclusive cultural diversity that is present in the twenty-first century. When we perpetually mourn the good old days, we fail to speak to the contemporary realities of life. Yes, those involved in neo-traditionalism can reformulate tradition for new purposes, crafting new institutional solutions that enjoy the benefit of social familiarity and embeddedness in local culture. But shaping congregations that connect with contemporary people in truly effective ways demands an understanding not simply of how culture and vision are recrafted, but that also asks: Who does the recrafting? How is power exercised? What interests are we pursuing? It is good to look back to the key lessons of the past, but we must interpret the modern-day applications of the past, not stay stuck in the past, especially given the history of racism, sexism, and classism in the United States. Depending on your social status or identity, the good old days may not have been that good. The gospel is for all, not just a select few.

Neo-traditionalists put their faith and that of others in danger when they ground the intellectual viability of the church on the idea that the church's teaching has never changed. While the church should not be held captive by popular culture, it must find ways to respond to the changing impact of culture on people. When neo-traditionalist churches allow themselves to be guided by a romanticized view of the past, they lose power and purpose.

Contemporary church leaders would be better served by reflecting on the Sankofa bird as a model of integrating the past with the future. *Sankofa* is an African word from the Akan people in Ghana that literally means "it is not taboo to fetch what is at risk of being left behind." The word is derived from the words *san* (return), *ko* (go), *fa* (look, seek, and take). The symbol of the Sankofa bird is a stylized drawing of a bird whose feet are grounded and pointed forward, and whose head is turned back yet remains alert to what lies ahead. The Sankofa bird reminds us that we must continue to move forward as we remember our past, planting seeds for the generations that come after us. The activated church builds on the foundation and lessons of the past but continues to advance and cultivate future generations.

What is the cause of the increasing marginalization of the church in American communities? It would be easy for me to get on my high horse and say, "The problem is that most church leaders stink." That wouldn't be helpful, and I am pretty sure I can't place a "laughing out loud" emoticon in this book to ease the tension that statement would create. As church leaders, most of us are committed and faithful. Depending on where we are in our leadership journey, we may feel deeply discouraged about dwindling congregations and the increasing marginalization of the church in the surrounding culture. We are tasked with leading in a culture that seems to no longer value church participation. We know God is faithful and that we are working harder than ever at the job of ministry, even as fewer and fewer people join our congregations. Depending on our demographics, those who do join are much more likely to be in their seventies than in their twenties. And to the next generation, membership is less likely to translate into regular participation in worship. It's clear that the church must change.

Several factors have contributed to the decrease in church attendance among Americans. One factor is that our sense of community, which was traditionally rooted in faith communities, is increasingly found in new social locations. I define community as a group of people who share common attributes that create strong, lasting bonds and a sense of belonging that guides and shapes behavior. Our understanding of community also shapes our values. The new centers of community for many in the younger generations are sports, school and its related activities, and the Internet. For most younger people, the church is not the center of community activity, even on Sundays. Club sports and traveling teams take families away from Sunday church attendance. Increasing debt and changes in family structure also affect the traditional Sunday morning service, as families burnt out by trying to make ends meet find that they lack motivation to hop in the car and attend an early morning worship service.

The transient nature of our society is another factor that has affected the church. If the beginning of the twentieth century was marked by the growth of the city and the mid to late twentieth century was marked by the growth of the suburbs, the beginning of the twenty-first century is marked by a return to the city. Geographic mobility has a direct impact on the growth potential and sustainability of a church. A 150-year-old church building cannot be picked up and moved, but families do move as young people follow jobs and societal movements. What was once a thriving populace in 1995 might be a community faced with a dying economy in 2021.

In our work and social relationships, Americans engage each other differently than we did in the past. We are broadly much more transient than generations past, and we are experiencing an increased isolation in many communities, where it's less common to know our neighbors. Because of how the world changed in 2020, we now know that developments in communication and software technology can create a sustainable form of community. Before COVID-19, we thought it was just the younger generations who consumed and "stayed put," forming online relationships. Now we are all seeing that it is possible to sustain long-term relationships with people who live in geographically distant locations. We no longer need to live and work in the same place. We do not have to see people or appear in person in order to feed ourselves, educate ourselves, or earn a living. The ability to work remotely decreases the importance of living near an office park or of forming relationships that take us to a physical church building. Some might argue that the social needs the church used to meet are no longer germane, because of the changes in our culture. Instead, I'd argue that we are connecting in many different ways in the twenty-first century, including through groups such as online potlucks.

In prior generations, there was often social pressure for some demographic groups to just "do" church. A white friend told me a story of her grandparents, who were not particularly God-loving people, but were adamant about attending church regularly in the 1950s. She reflects that their church membership likely had more to do with assimilating as new immigrants, seeking middle-class respectability, and creating social connections than it did with Christian conviction. Nowadays, people join country clubs, service organizations, book clubs, sports groups, and professional organizations to meet those same needs. You can even belong to these groups virtually. In this sense, what has changed is not the church, but the values of the surrounding culture.

For other Americans, church provided a refuge that could be found in few other spaces. For my family, and for many people of color, participation in the church was not so much about seeking status as it was about seeking safety, justice, and hope. Now, because of the civil rights movement, improved communication systems, and the increasing affluence of people of color, the church is not the only safe refuge, and some of the reverence paid to clergy as icons of communities of color is fading.

I asked Candace, a female millennial friend of mine, why she thinks the church is no longer relevant. Candace does not attend church but did attend as a youth and has a strong Christian background. She responded, "I think most churches historically that had greater relevance than they do now were centers of social activity. They were in smaller communities, and so it was like a melting chamber for many different parts of the community. So I think if churches want to become more relevant, they need to understand the current issues of the community, not just serving the poor, which is obviously important. Not just saving your souls, but helping shape the world, even speaking into politics as appropriate." Candace's perspective supports my understanding of the cultural shifts that have affected American society in recent decades, especially in the Black community. Candace even gave a nod to the impact the church formerly had on influencing social change through movements such as the civil rights movement, equating relevance with some type of social transformation. But Candace also acknowledged that the communities we are a part of today are much different. Our geographic transience means we are more spread out from the people with whom we have the closest bonds, and our ability to maintain relationships digitally means we often remain more emotionally detached from our actual neighbors in our local communities.

Finally, an increasing distrust of institutions in American culture has also contributed to a decline in church participation. People have more access to information, and this has forced transparency that did not exist in years past. It is more challenging for church leaders who abuse power to cover up scandals. The church is a place where adults and children should feel safe; today's leaders must recognize and acknowledge the damage that has been done related to sexual abuse and the abuse of power. When people lose trust and are abused by the church, they stop coming, and the church loses not only that person, but several generations of their family.

From time to time we must be reminded that we are children of the light. Ephesians 5:14 calls us to wake up so that the light of Christ will shine on us. I believe in the church and its leaders. There are many leaders who are already wide awake, doing all that is good, right, and true. But even the best of us get drowsy from time to time and need a little nudge. The awakened churches are beacons of hope. They are helping provide comfort, shelter, and assistance to many both inside and outside of their congregation. It is my hope that every congregation and every Christian leader wakes up fully to become an imitator of Christ. "Therefore be imitators of God, as beloved children, and live in love, as Christ loved us and gave himself up for us, a fragrant offering and sacrifice to God" (Ephesians 5:1-2).

So what is a reawakened church, one that is activated to spark lasting change? And what do leaders and champions of the next generation of the church need to lead activated churches? Based on my conversations, observations, and almost twenty-five years of working in ministry, I have identified several key characteristics that successful, activated congregations have in common.

First, an activated church leads, meaning that it actively seeks to understand the community, adapting when appropriate and challenging the community when appropriate. I liken the mission of the activated church to the sending of the twelve disciples in Luke 9:1-6. The activated church knows that it is dependent on the community, just as Jesus called the disciples to depend on those they served for their daily needs. Sometimes we are called to sit at the table; at other times, we are called to shake the dust of an unwelcoming community off our feet. Regardless, the activated church is always about the business of preaching the gospel and healing the wounded for the sake of leading people toward transformation.

Second, an activated church increasingly demonstrates eight key characteristics. The activated church enacts the following behaviors or activities:

1. Has a clear understanding of its *identity* in the community.
2. Practices *mission-focused spirituality*, which allows it to see the needs of the community and to respond appropriately.
3. Enacts an intentional strategy for *discipleship and faith formation*.
4. Develops and relates to a *diverse Christian community*, facilitating an interculturally competent community.
5. Develops *strategic community partnerships* that help fulfill the great commandment by fostering health, hope, and healing.
6. Understands and lives out a *holistic witness* in its context.
7. Practices and teaches *sound stewardship* principles, helping members see money and personal resources as tools to bless the entire community.
8. Has a long-term plan for *leadership development* that values the gifts of every person, models good leadership practices, and prepares for leader succession.

Will the activated church do everything perfectly? Of course not. But activated churches will work at each of the characteristics in a meaningful way.

Activated congregations and leaders have been a part of the church from its beginning. As the early church expanded, it brought together many different cultures. The encounter between Philip and the Ethiopian in Acts 8:26-39 highlights the powerful transformation that can occur when the church engages those outside its cultural bubble. Philip and the Ethiopian were prompted by the Spirit to embark on journeys that led their paths to collide. The Ethiopian man was reading Isaiah 53, which provided Philip the opportunity to explain and preach to him about the Messiah, Jesus Christ. The Bible study led to the baptism of this influential Ethiopian dignitary, who worked for Candace, the queen of the Ethiopians. The two men from a hodgepodge of cultural backgrounds and traditions came together, led by the Spirit. According to church tradition, the Ethiopian took his newfound faith with him back to his home region, building a foundation for the church that would, in the fourth century, witness the conversion of the Ethiopian king and the creation of a Christian kingdom.

This Ethiopian is an archetype of the transitional leader we need today, a bridge between cultures who can unite us in Christ, and without which the activated church does not exist. The early church grew in power and relevance because it so easily transcended barriers of culture and tradition. The activated church leader is like the Ethiopian eunuch—curious, brave, and willing to adventure beyond cultural constraints to grasp the good news fully. The eunuch was also conscious enough of his own culture that he was able to help facilitate its transformation. Like him, we need to power up our ministry for community engagement and transformative discipleship.

As I researched this book, in addition to drawing on my own experience in ministry, I sought wisdom and perspectives on leading effectively in our current cultural context from a variety of pastors and church leaders. A few years back, I started asking a series of analytical questions about what makes people and systems successful:

- What makes some churches very connected to the pulse of their community, while others seem isolated and disconnected?

- What makes individual churches from the same denomination successful, while others fail?

- If I was new to the faith and starting over, what would it take to reach me? (I think Christian leaders always need to ask themselves some variation of this question. "If I wasn't the pastor or a leader, would I join this church?")

As I sought answers to these questions, I started meeting with leaders in my community and with other Black, Indigenous, and people of color (BIPOC) pastors. These were older, seasoned pastors with years of urban and community-based ministry experience.

I am part of the Mennonite church, but as a Black man, I am an ethnic outsider in a historically white denomination that has strong ethnic roots in Swiss-German, German, and Dutch immigrant communities. My faith journey was directly affected and altered by the Mennonites. This strange yet rewarding journey has led me to become the first African American and first non-ethnic Mennonite to serve as the executive director of Mennonite Church USA. Many Mennonites in North America share a traceable central European ancestry. It is not uncommon for convinced Anabaptists to draw some distinction between their faith journey and the journey of those with ethnic roots, sometimes called "cradle" Mennonites. For some the moniker of Anabaptist helps to clarify that distinction of choosing to become a part of the faith tradition versus being "born into" fellowship.

BIPOC Mennonite congregations provide a particularly fruitful place for seeking answers to these questions, in part because many of them have been able to weather the storms of lack, while changing social demographics are new experiences for the more traditional ethnically European white congregations that now are shrinking in both size and influence. Mennonites have been traditionally isolated from mainstream culture, even though they agree that church planting and evangelism should be priorities of the church. Conrad Kanagy, a Mennonite sociologist, found that 88 percent of Mennonites believed that "Christians should do all they can to convert all non-believers to Christ."[4] Because of this interest in evangelism and church planting, the Mennonite church has seen significant growth of BIPOC Mennonite congregations in urban areas. Although the cultural differences are stark between Mennonites who identify ethnically with their European-immigrant forebears and those who have come to Anabaptism strictly because of Anabaptist theology, the outward focus of Mennonite spirituality drew many urban leaders from diverse ethnic backgrounds into the Mennonite faith during a time when Mennonites were mainly thought of as rural farmers. Kanagy has observed that "the growth of racial/ethnic congregations is changing the face of Mennonite Church USA."[5] These racial/ethnic Mennonite congregations in urban areas have a strong religious yet robust ethnic identity that provides a particularly good place to begin looking for answers to questions about why some churches of the same denomination succeed while others fail.

Urban ministry can be rewarding, but it comes with its own unique set of challenges. In urban areas, diverse people, cultures, and customs come together in a critical mass, but this does not always form a synergetic harmony. Urban communities have class extremes, with the rich and poor living in proximity to one another. In a dense city, doctors and lawyers may live a few blocks from dockworkers and bricklayers. There are also issues of communication. One neighbor may speak Korean, one may speak Spanish, and another may speak Indonesian. We should not minimize the problems of social and religious heterogeneity that need to be addressed before any relevant ministry can occur in an urban context. Most churches must figure out how to preach the gospel to first-time seekers, but imagine trying to teach about Christ to a room filled with Muslims, Hindus, Buddhists, and nominal Christians.

While the density, diversity, and heterogeneity of the urban setting can be challenging, there is an upside to ministry in an urban setting—namely, an abundance of people. In the urban environment, there is never an absence of people. There are thriving multigenerational homes and people living in exceptionally dense neighborhoods. As people come together, there is a fantastic amalgamation of cultures and understandings that form something distinct and new. Often, because of the significant needs and scarcity of resources in some urban communities, there is a hunger for good news—a longing for the gospel of peace. Urban dwellers understand that to survive, everyone must find common ground and develop new ways to live as one. Despite the pain that urban communities sometimes face, my experience as an African American and as a global traveler is that it is often in these places, which have seen the most pain and conflict, that people are most open to the hope of Christ.

As noted, I interviewed a variety of pastors and church leaders for this book. I selected these leaders for their entrepreneurial drive and impact on their community beyond the traditional Sunday morning service. They all have engaged at some point in the "traditional" forms of church, such as the Sunday and midweek model of meeting, but they are all also involved in engaging their broader community, whether through community activism, church planting, school clubs, or partnerships with parachurch groups that are intentionally reaching out to people beyond the congregation. The leaders I interviewed come from a variety of Christian faith traditions, ages, educational backgrounds, and church sizes, and represent a diverse group of church leaders. One congregation has a membership of sixty people; another has fourteen hundred members. I even interviewed a church planter who was just starting to build a ministry team. But each of the leaders whom I interviewed had a track record of connecting with their community beyond worship services and outside the physical church building.

I intentionally interviewed millennials and Gen Xers because they are the leaders who are gaining increased responsibility in the church as the baby boomers retire. The older urban leaders inspired me, but I wanted to reach out to the next generation, to those who would be most likely to carry the torch forward. Even so, I did not want to discount the wisdom of the prior generations, and I wanted to test the responses of the younger generations against the wisdom of their elders. I have what I think is a good foundation in leadership wisdom, but it is important to ensure that those lessons are transferable to the next generation. I am a firm believer that good leadership transcends generations. We must always pay attention to culture and context, including technology, but good leadership principles have longevity.

As I embarked upon the journey of writing this book, I had Generation Y/millennials and Generation Z in mind, because they include the young families and young people who must carry the church forward. These generations include both the kids I mentored as a youth pastor and my own children. I've wrestled with a lot of questions about these generations. What are their views on Christianity and church as they move into adulthood and begin to fill the roles of teachers and leaders? How can we make the church great again, or at least relevant in their eyes?

This book is written for the next generation of church leaders, those who will call themselves pastors to the millennials and Gen Zers. My hope is that you, reader, are part of the transitional generation of church leaders who will take us from the structured corporate-centered leadership of the baby boomers to the more people- and mission-centered leadership that will engage the twenty-first-century Christian. I also hope this book will be helpful to older readers who are able to shift and respond to the needs of the next great generation. For readers starting a ministry from scratch, this book will be an excellent blueprint to help you build your ministry from the ground up, beginning with key characteristics of an activated church in mind. For the seasoned leader, I hope this book gives you the tools and support you need to be able to shift the culture of church.

The successful, thriving urban churches that I studied and have experienced myself all possess several similar characteristics. And while the model I present in this book is based on successful urban churches, I believe that the lessons learned can provide a robust framework for suburban and even rural churches to become reawakened in their own contexts.

I believe in the church, its power, and its importance to our communities. The activated church has a crucially important role in the well-being of our communities and our nation. Is your church awakened for ministry that can spark change, or is it in danger of being dumped on the scrap heap? Is your congregation's ministry a healing presence in the community in which you serve? Here are a few questions to ask yourself to determine the relevancy of your congregation:

1. *Does your church have a heart to serve others?* Does your church function like a weekend country club for the privileged few, or is there an outward focus to your faith community? I have seen too many island churches taking up real estate in their community without affecting the community. The activated church is not driven to just please people, but is an influencer of people and part of the pulse of the community it serves.

2. *Does your congregation focus on helping members grow, or does it focus on what it can get from people?* Declining churches think in terms of what they can get from members—money,

time, prestige, and so on. Members of these churches are often guilted into supporting the ministry. The members are used by their leaders, like sheep that are "sheared" weekly. The refrain of these churches is often "Give, give, give so that you can be blessed, blessed, blessed." Personal blessings and transformation are connected to tithes and offering, not life change. It is as if the pastors of these churches are mimicking the thought control of the abusive teacher in the Pink Floyd song who warns that if you do not eat the meat, there will not be any pudding for you. Their refrain might be, "If you don't give more money, you can't have your blessings." In contrast, activated churches think about the future and how they will build people up or increase the capacity of their members and the community. They create passion around service, community, and generosity, where Christ is at the center of everyone's life.

3. *Can people easily get involved?* Large bureaucracies don't spur innovation in business, and they don't work in churches either. By innovation, I mean passion and creativity that attract other passionate and creative people and allow them to use their strengths. Innovation involves more than gathering creative and passionate people—it involves their creation of new ways of doing things. While the activated church needs to vet people and be strategic in selecting leaders, it also needs to function as an effective distribution center. The activated church should be a place where people can be grounded and centered while sharing their gifts inside and outside of the church. Unnecessary church bureaucracy and control are barriers to people serving and staying connected. Later in this book, I will share some business-inspired principles, but I don't believe those to be contradictory to my current point. I am not saying that churches should not have controls and a system, but rather that the way a church operates should always help the congregation achieve its mission. The policy manual for a church should never replace

the leading of the Holy Spirit. We want churches that attract creative and passionate people and that empower them (or at least don't impede them with bureaucracy) in their quest to exercise their creativity.

4. *Is your congregation seen as a resource provider during times of crisis?* The activated church, through its stewardship of resources or its strategic partnerships, will be a place of refuge, if not for all challenges, then for those challenges most likely to affect its core community.

5. *What is your congregation's orientation to justice?* The activated church is justice-oriented. Dr. Martin Luther King Jr. said this best when he quoted Amos 5:24, "Let justice roll down like waters and righteousness like a mighty stream." A few hymns quote that passage as well. Feel free to hum a few bars before reading on. Some aspect of your ministry should be serving the marginalized, the oppressed, or the underserved.

Keep reading and we'll explore this together.

ONE

The Activated Church

*I also pray that you will understand the incredible
greatness of God's power for us who believe him....*
—EPHESIANS 1:19 (NLT)

THE POWER AND PURPOSE OF THE CHURCH

What is the power of the church? The power of the church is
not found in its icons, its hierarchy, or its bureaucracy. The real
power of the church lies in its ability to transfer the hopes and
dreams of its lowest members into action. Simply put, the power
of the church lies in transformation. While transformation
will look different in different communities and with different
people the church serves, the mission of the church is always
to prepare people for transformation to happen. This power
is illustrated in the books of Ezra and Nehemiah. Professor
Andrew Hill writes, "The labors of Ezra and Nehemiah to rebuild and reform postexilic Jerusalem was largely inspired by
the theological truth of Yahweh as covenant keeper."[1] Ezra and
Nehemiah illustrated unwavering hope and certainty through
which a marginalized community was able to center itself and

rebuild. While individuals had specific roles and duties in the process, the institution of religion helped lay the foundation for the restoration and rebuilding of the community.

If you had asked me as a young pastor some twenty-five years ago to name the mission of the church, I would have said that our mission as a church, no matter how we try to complexify it, is to share the good news, the gospel. The New Testament makes it abundantly clear that Christ is both the foundation (Acts 4:11-12; 1 Corinthians 3:11) and the head (Ephesians 5:23) of the church. Sharing the gospel, in word and action, provides hope necessary for people to believe and to receive all that God has to offer them. That definition is close to what I believe now, but it confuses the mission with methodology. The traditional preaching of the gospel is only one step in the process of transformation. We are called not only to proclaim the Word, but to deeds of discipleship and healing of hurts.

The activated church taps into the power of the Spirit and the more tangible networks of the community to restore the hopes and dreams of people, opening them up to the possibility of transformation.

One other conviction that I have continued to hold since I was a young pastor is that what we do as a Christian church should be very simple. People need to have a deep understanding of what the gospel means to Christians, so churches should not simplify it. But we do need to streamline church bureaucracy, and to remove all the non-value-added steps that can make serving a church feel like signing up for a thirty-year mortgage. We need simple, repeatable processes that will help us activate our churches to become centers of transformation. By simple, I mean simplicity in the ways we engage people, the ease of which we make decisions, and how quickly we can mobilize to meet the needs of the community. We are often tempted to equate complexity with good management and accountability. Churches have fallen into the trap of thinking that complexity makes ministry better. It doesn't. Simplicity should be our goal. Can you imagine if Jesus needed all the boards and subcommittees our churches have today? He never would have been able to perform his first miracle at Cana. It would have taken ten boards, the hospitality committee, and a congregational vote to determine if it was okay for him to serve wine, and three more months of meetings to determine the alcohol content and type of wine.

In their book, *Simple Church*, Thom Rainer and Eric Geiger write, "In general, simple churches are growing and vibrant. . . . Conversely, complex churches are struggling and anemic."[2] They interviewed over four hundred evangelical churches, comparing vibrant growing churches and nongrowing struggling churches. Simplicity wins. I appreciate the model Rainer and Geiger outline: Clarity. Movement. Alignment. Focus. While this book does not speak directly to their model, if you practice the characteristics of successfully activated churches, you will be in line with their principles.

Many of our American churches today have confused offering programming with the mission of transformation. Focusing on programming and infrastructure has distracted us from focusing on the purpose of the church. We equate spiritual health, well-being, and transformation with attendance, budget, and social media engagements—the same metrics used by your local health club or movie theater. While church services can be entertaining and many churches even have cafés, these offerings do not speak to the reason the church was breathed into existence on the day of Pentecost.

"But you will receive power when the Holy Spirit has come upon you; and you will be my witnesses in Jerusalem, in all Judea and Samaria, and to the ends of the earth." In Acts 1:8, Jesus did not tell the disciples, "Go build big expensive buildings, and then constantly beg for money so that you can have the greatest youth group and Christmas musical in all of Albuquerque." If we are honest, many institutionalized churches have so crippled themselves with the bureaucracy and business of religion that they can no longer afford to do mission. They must keep their clients happy to ensure that their clients keep giving and keep coming to the often-underutilized structural edifices that have incredibly high operating costs. As I visit churches across the country, I see many churches that are more like mini malls. A few of the businesses run by local congregations include day-cares, coffee shops, merry-go-rounds, event space, schools, restaurants, gymnasiums, splash parks, and thrift stores.

Is it wrong for churches to include all these businesses? Not necessarily. If a church wants to spend a few hundred thousand dollars on a water park and a coffee shop, I have no problem with it. But regardless of the program or project, my question will always be, "Is this intentionally designed to bring transformation to the lives of the people in your community?" We need to ask that question for every program or project we undertake in ministry. One thing I am learning from interviewing younger pastors and leaders is that the church of the future must pay attention to the needs of the community. A message centered on prohibitions is not going to change the world. People want genuine relationships, not bureaucracy and barriers.

Transformation can happen on many levels and in numerous ways. Ultimately, we want people to have a spiritual transformation as described in Romans 12:2, which calls us to "be transformed by the renewing of your minds." But the church can also provide transformation in the areas of education, poverty reduction, physical and mental wellness, family relationships, community relationships, and social justice (life, liberty, and the pursuit of happiness). Based on the community that you serve, you may need to address one or more of these needs. The activated church understands that spiritual transformation will not happen without addressing the underlying needs of people. Poverty, homelessness, classism, racism, and economic deprivation all create hopelessness.

It is the Holy Spirit who dwells in us and brings about transformation. The transformation I am talking about happening in and through the church isn't just a positive, feel-good moment—which is something any well-run community organization could effect. There is something about spiritual transformation that is much deeper; it's unique. It brings a peaceful relief, lasting liberty. The Holy Spirit is at the heart of it, bringing it about—and when the church joins the Spirit in that transformation, we are enfolded into the transforming life of God. I remember seeing my daughter being born. It broke me. I cried as I never had before with tears of joy. I have been crying for twenty-three years since then. I can't stop. Every time I watch a movie about a father and their kids, I turn into mush, and it is my daughter's fault. The transformation of the Holy Spirit is like that. It changes you in ways you did not think were possible.

Being an activated church that is at the center of transformation means breaking out of old paradigms. It means casting off cultural bondage (often wrapped in theology) and paying attention to the message of Christ through a fresh lens. The activated church should cast off any bias or church tradition that does not line up with the Word of God. This is what sixteenth-century German theologian Hans Denck called us to when he wrote, "Holy Scripture I hold above all human treasure but not as high as the Word of God that is living, powerful and eternal—unattached and free of all elements of this world; for, since it is God himself, it is Spirit and not letter, written without pen and paper so that it can never be eradicated. Therefore, salvation is not bound to Scripture, however useful and good it might be in furthering it. . . . But a devout heart, containing a true spark of divine zeal, is improved through all things." Denck is warning of legalistic religion based on a "dead letter." Denck is warning us against having a dead, culturally incompetent interpretation of Scripture. He is concerned that biblical legalism will lead God's children down the wrong path. "Seeking light," they will "find darkness." Transformation happens in the light of hope that the activated church shines through its connection to the community, which it serves.

WHY DO WE ALL NEED TRANSFORMATION?

Transformation is synonymous with growth, and everything that is alive should experience growth. Transformation happens when we build on our knowledge and our experiences, and we take that information to live out our purpose, our call. A call is a summons to a specific course of action, influenced by the divine. Transformation happens when we are able not only to live our lives, but to love the lives that we live—when we can attach the gift of our lives to a higher purpose. We can see how our lives connect to something bigger than ourselves. Most, if not all, of us need that transformation to thrive. *If we don't understand our life's purpose when answering that divine call and if we lose our sense of self, we wind up like the walking dead (pun intended).* We are in a zombie-like state of being, wandering, with no destination in mind, and no vision. When we don't have a sense of self, like zombies, we just move in the direction that someone or something else points us toward. That someone or something else might be social media, the regular media, drugs, or some random person we hook up with at a party. We wander and wander, and we do this until we eventually die. We just quit, we give up, experiencing both a metaphorical and literal death.

ARTICULATE THAT THE CHURCH IS A PLACE OF TRANSFORMATION

The Spirit empowers our communities to embody the grace, joy, and peace of the gospel. The church is part of that process.

I believe, especially in the United States, that the church has failed to demonstrate why it is needed. Like the character in the Monty Python skit, we keep hollering, "I'm alive, I'm alive," but the culture around us keeps bopping us on the head and saying, "Nope, you're dead. You're not relevant." By "relevant," I mean a faith community that can facilitate the transformation that is most needed by the people and community we serve. We have failed to tell our story in a way that lets people realize that the church is still a viable place of healing and hope that leads to transformation. Why aren't more folks relating transformation to what we do as the church?

People are looking for more government intervention. More and more secular nonprofits are popping up to serve the needs of the marginalized. According to the National Center of Charitable Statistics, the nonprofit sector has grown by 20 percent throughout the last decade. If anything, the church is saying in some cases, "Fix yourself. Don't bring your mess, your sin into our pristine community." People know they are struggling with various issues of life. They don't believe the church is the place that can happen. Rather than allowing people to come to church as they are, which often is broken, confused, and in need of purpose, we expect them to come pure, clean, and white as snow (yes, in many places, whiteness or white culture is still the equivalent of holiness). We force a false purity on them, so they hide their brokenness, their needs, and the gaps in their lives that need filling. We are not helping them prepare for the indwelling of the Holy Spirit.

WE NEED TO SHIFT THE MESSAGE OF THE TRANSFORMATION BROUGHT ABOUT THROUGH THE CHURCH

One key is helping people understand that without Christ, the transformation they obtain may be temporary. What do we do as the Christian church that is unique and special? Before we try to force people to understand that they need transformation, we need to articulate the benefits of that transformation. We have to share the peace it brings. I promise you that the purity proposition is not going to work effectively for the people of today. Standing in the street and yelling, "You're going to hell, repent!" will not motivate or captivate a community (even if it is full of sinners going to hell). Unsolicited condemnations are not value-added propositions, and some people might think the life they live is already hell.

People in our communities need real change, real hope, real help, today. For a twenty-five-year-old who is full of life, hell-fire and the dread of eternal damnation are not going to be big motivators for looking at life differently. As church leaders, we understand the theology of heaven and hell, but when folks are living to eighty years of age and are popping Viagra like candy, they probably think they can put off Jesus for a year or two and go live their lives. Is the only reason we are telling people to follow Christ so that they can go the heaven when they die? Is that it? Is that the good news we want to share for people to experience this spiritual transformation?

YOU CAN'T LEGISLATE TRANSFORMATION

Some churches attempt to bring about transformation through legalism, especially in youth-related ministry. I have worked with Christian schools and youth groups who have tried to legislate purity. They have put processes in place to keep young people from having premarital sex. The method comes in the form of gender-segregated activities, segregated buses to camp, segregated seating, et cetera. This is an exercise in futility for the following reasons: No one can watch kids twenty-four hours a day. You must eat, sleep, and go to the bathroom. And separation on a bus does not fix issues of the heart or influence what kids do the rest of the time when they are out of your sight. Furthermore, today's youth are more open with other types of relationships. Gender segregation does not consider same-gender relationships. Ultimately, gender segregation sends the message that age-appropriate transformation is not possible and that sexual relationships are our master. Many of the actions put in place disproportionally disempower young women. Churches create an environment where young girls and women become ashamed of their bodies, or they come to think of young men as unguided, heat-seeking sexualized weapons.

Our role is to guide young people, not to surround them in spiritual bubble wrap. Do you have to watch young people? Yes. Do you have to save them from making poor decisions? Absolutely. But the segregation model does not lead young people to a place of mature spiritual transformation. It would be better for church leaders to put in place accountability checks and balances and to create an environment for young people to grow, ask questions, and think through the decisions they make. Some examples of procedures that foster accountability and monitored growth include lessons in self-esteem, meeting in larger groups versus dyads, gathering in open spaces rather than behind closed doors, instituting a "one blanket, one person" rule, offering workshops on developing a healthy identity, teaching youth to communicate and respect consent, studying biblical relationships, exposing youth to positive adult role models, and asking youth to follow a mutually agreed-upon code of conduct that they help shape.

Transformation shows up in the following ways:

The fruit we produce. "By contrast, the fruit of the Spirit is love, joy, peace, patience, kindness, generosity, faithfulness, gentleness, and self-control. There is no law against such things" (Galatians 5:22-23).

When transformation happens in the lives of people, we see tangible changes in their choices, their behavior, and their environment. They begin to live their lives differently. They can let go of addictions and unhealthy habits that controlled them in the past.

The voice we recognize. "My sheep hear my voice. I know them, and they follow me" (John 10:27).

Transformation allows us to see and hear the world differently. The voice of the Holy Spirit nudges us in the right direction and cuts through the daily noise of life. One would hope that as we truly experience transformation, we would see ourselves as sojourners with a godly assignment and not as ideological factions. The untransformed mind is easily distracted and can be moved off its divine path by any number of bright and shiny objects. When we hear from God we may not have the same clarity as the prophet Samuel, but if we want to feel successful and fulfilled, at some point we all must say yes to our calling. A single calling can lead you down many paths. The transformed mind recognizes and responds to one's true calling. It does not get distracted by every bright and shiny opportunity that comes along, spiritual or otherwise.

The Spirit we trust. "But the Advocate, the Holy Spirit, whom the Father will send in my name, will teach you everything, and remind you of all that I have said to you" (John 14:26).

As the leader of a religious denomination, I often remind people that salvation does not come from our documents or our bureaucratic religious systems. As Christians, we must always trust the Spirit over any human social legislation. Transformation should provide a sense of peace that at the end of the day, God, not us, is in control. Sure, churches and religious organizations need to be run well and to have sound systems in place. But what often happens is that we trust more in our governing boards, lawyers, and policy manuals than in the Spirit. The transformed church pays attention to the movement of God in the world and responds to it.

The grace we give. "Each time he said, 'My grace is all you need. My power works best in weakness.' So now I am glad to boast about my weaknesses, so that the power of Christ can work through me" (2 Corinthians 12:9 NLT).

Part of transformation involves an acceptance not only of the faults of others but also of our own.

The faith we experience. A few of my Latinx friends claim that Spanish is the language of heaven (insert eye roll emoji here). I lovingly reject their arrogant declaration, but for some reason, some expressions of faith do sound better to me in Spanish. One of my favorite hymns, "La montaña" ("The Mountain"), as performed by the band Salvador, talks about faith in the following way:

> Si tuvieras fe como grano de mostaza,
> eso lo dice el Señor,
> tu le dirías a la montaña,
> Muévete, muévete,
> esa montaña se movera,
> se movera, se movera

The hymn is a musical rendition of Matthew 17:20. If we have *fe* (faith) the size of a grain of a mustard seed, we command the mountain to *muévete* (move), and it will move. That is a sure sign of transformation when we can take control of the mountains and obstacles and speak them out of our path. As I reflect on the meaning of the Scripture, I don't see transformation making our problems disappear so much as making our problems no longer capable of hindering us on our journey. Sin and the cares of this world block our ability to see the power and presence of God in our lives, but faith, according to Scripture, is built a foundation of hope and needs no visual evidence to prove itself true (Hebrews 11:1). With our transformation, there should be a change and strengthening of our faith. We should not fear problems as much as we should begin to embrace the ability of the power of God to help us overcome. Part of that power comes from the collective community that we join. Some of the help we receive will be earthly based.

Community transformation is seen in the following:

The goodness we share. "The point is this: the one who sows sparingly will also reap sparingly, and the one who sows bountifully will also reap bountifully. Each of you must give as you have made up your mind, not reluctantly or under compulsion, for God loves a cheerful giver. And God is able to provide you with every blessing in abundance, so that by always having enough of everything, you may share abundantly in every good work" (2 Corinthians 9:6-8).

The grace that we accept. "But each of us was given grace according to the measure of Christ's gift" (Ephesians 4:7).

When we genuinely experience transformation, we realize that Christ has given us a gift. We did not earn forgiveness, and we cannot pay it back. We embrace the gift without guilt or shame. The mature Christian understands that works don't earn us the love of God; the mature Christian also knows we must extend that same grace to others. Many people who are outside of the church feel judged by those who are inside the church. There is something in their minds or perhaps in the behavior of the church that suggests that before you can become a part of the body, you must be perfectly clean. One of the old hymns talks about the blood of Christ removing all the guilty stains of sinners. For years, whenever I heard that song, my thoughts immediately went to Christ washing away my sins and creating this new sinless individual. Now, as I think about that old hymn and transformation, I see Christ's removal of the "guilt" of sin as part of the process. It allows us to feel worthy of moving forward.

Healing and meeting basic human needs are part of the transformation process. If we are not actively engaged in lifting others, I would question whether we have genuinely experienced transformation. Sharing is caring, as they say, and it is also an excellent sign of transformation. Look at nature. When the butterfly emerges from its cocoon, it flies from flower to flower, helping pollinate plants. The same with bees—as they work and live their lives, they spread pollen to our crops. They make honey, and they feed the world in several ways. They can't help it. That is how we should live our lives and run our churches. As we work and do ministry, we should infect and influence the community around us. We should not be isolated islands of refuge. We should be like emergent butterflies, fully engaged, spreading the seeds of growth and hope in our communities.

Transformation does take time. There are no shortcuts. In the natural world, we understand that growth and maturity happen over long periods. When someone in our family brings home a newborn baby, our expectations for its contributions to the family are very different from the expectations we have for a teenager. As the parent of two children, I tried to match my expectations to both their age and mental growth, as well as to their personalities. As my son grew older, I only expected him to brush his teeth and wash his face each morning. That was a significant accomplishment, especially for him. Now that he is a young adult, he takes out the trash, drives me to the airport, and is responsible for managing his college finances. When my daughter was sixteen, it was a challenge for me to allow her to drive a car or go places by herself. I worried about her, and I wanted to protect her. Since then she has moved to Los Angeles, worked as an intern, and become a flight attendant. She travels by herself and is considering going to nursing school to care for others. There is a growth process in the natural world and the spiritual world as well. It takes time for people to mature in Christ. It takes time to learn new habits, and even to understand the culture of organizations such as the church. There are ups and downs, trial and error, mistakes and successes. For twenty-plus years, I mentored and guided each of my children in a safe and secure environment to prepare them for adulthood. Why can't that happen within the church with the spiritually immature and those who may have never before known Christ? The church should not be simply a place of judgment; it should be an incubator that produces mature, healthy disciples.

WHAT TRANSFORMATION IS NOT

Transformation is not a change brought about by doing good deeds or having perfect behavior. Consider someone who is sick and blemished. Imagine that person just put on makeup to look better and hide the flaws. The concealing powder improves one's appearance, but it does not make one healthier. Below the surface, the problems still exist. The change is superficial. Genuine healing comes as a result of a change in the life process within.

The church must inspire and guide its members to not only adjust their external behavior (makeup) but change what is within. Transformation is not merely about imitating Christ's life the best we can. Genuine conversion is different. An inward change takes place in our being as we receive Christ as our spiritual food and drink. In transformation, we embody Christ. We become filled with and are one with the Spirit, the *ruah* of God. As the Spirit fills us, the divine life within us can operate, and our "appearance" gradually improves until we symbiotically begin to express Christ more in our daily lives, just like a caterpillar that becomes a beautiful butterfly.

We can't transform ourselves, but we can "be transformed." The activated church is a place where that transformation can occur. It is not the only place of transformation, but the church should and must create an environment that presents the gospel and nurtures relationships in a way that people can say yes to the process.

QUESTIONS FOR REFLECTION

1. How does your congregation bring transformation to the community in which you serve?

2. How do you monitor people to know that transformation is happening?

3. What is the fruit your ministry produces?

4. What are some of the unmet needs in your community?

5. What project or program is preventing you from accomplishing your mission of transformation?

6. Are there church leaders or church systems that are hindering your ability to bring transformation to the community?

TWO

Seeker Friendly, SEO Savvy, or Something Else

Don't copy the behavior and customs of this world, but let God transform you into a new person by changing the way you think. Then you will learn to know God's will for you, which is good and pleasing and perfect.
—ROMANS 12:2 (NLT)

THE CHURCH NO LONGER plays the leading role in society that it once did.

We no longer follow the Old Testament model of a single sanctuary that housed the presence of God at the center of the community. In Israel, the idea of one sanctuary was symbolically related to the concept of one God, and to the theological belief in God's continual, unique presence in the temple in Jerusalem, which made it impossible for more than one shrine to be maintained. I wonder what gods divide our attention today and how that should shape the way we think about congregational life. If the reality of our community has changed and we think differently about what is central to our lives, how should those changes be reflected in the methodology that we use to "do" church? What idols have displaced God's presence at the center of our community? What rituals do we perform today? What is the symbolic center of our attention in our faith?

I called on a millennial youth pastor friend of mine to see what he thought of this concept of the changing center of our community and how it affected his ability to connect with youth and families.

Alex reflected, "In some ways, churches have become dinosaurs. We are five to seven years behind in technology. The computers are old and outdated, and we are not connecting with people where they are." He added, "Adults spend three to five hours on their phones [each day]. Some studies say teens spend seven to nine hours a day on their phones. So, when we think about connecting with families and youth, how can we ignore cell phones? That is the community in which they live."

I had to agree with Alex. In most of the churches I have led or attended, we have lagged in technology. Many churches were still making cassette tapes and door hangers, even as the world shifted to MP3s and email.

Alex continued, "You and everyone else is looking down at your iPhone or Android most of the day. It entertains you. It gives you the news, and everyone is pushing information to you. That is where the youth and everyone else lives. People would think I am crazy if I went around knocking on neighborhood doors unannounced, but the phone is the new door. The cell phone is a valid gateway to the community today."

Many churches define themselves through two things: membership and attendance. I do not think there is a magic

Figure 2. **Life cycle of the church community**

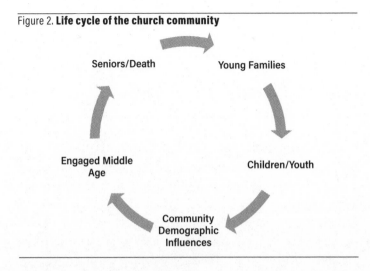

number for the ideal membership size. Jesus spent time with his three closest disciples, the twelve disciples, the seventy, and the crowd. Regardless of size, to be considered a church or a congregation, you have to have people, and whatever size you are, you must have a valid mission that you hope to accomplish. A mentor once told me that any healthy entity grows. Activated churches should show signs of life and growth.

Whatever the size of a congregation, it should represent the life cycle and demographics of the community. We will talk about the homogeneity of churches later, but in general, the activated church should reflect the community that surrounds it. A healthy church will minister to the community from birth to death, no matter the stage of life at which a member joins or whether that member completes their entire circle of life experience with the church.

One caveat about the size of congregations: LifeWay Research surveyed one thousand Protestant pastors in 2019 and rated and categorized churches into five categories, assessing how many fell into each group:[1]

1. Level 1: Subtracting   35 percent
2. Level 2: Plateauing   35 percent
3. Level 3: Adding   30 percent
4. Level 4: Reproducing   7 percent
5. Level 5: Multiplying   0 percent

All churches were placed in a growth context level (Levels 1, 2, and 3). Only 30 percent of the churches were in adding category, signifying some type of expansion. And on average, larger churches outperformed smaller churches in terms of growth. That is not to say that smaller churches were not experiencing growth, but larger churches have greater access to people and other resources. The survey defines small churches as congregations under fifty, which for most churches represents their size at either their beginning or ending point as a congregation. Of the total congregations surveyed only 7% rose to the reproduction level, meaning they were planting other churches. According to the survey methodology, "The metrics that qualify a church as reproducing require being substantially involved in starting new churches beyond being minimally or aspirationally involved. Functionally, the threshold of investment for Level 4 categorization is intended to be greater than that required for a typical church to simply add additional church services."[2]

The LifeWay study focuses on church multiplication and church planting. Church planting and multiplication are important, but in this book, I am more concerned about healthy, relevant churches as a starting point. We need more strong churches and not a bunch of struggling, ineffective ones.

Church attendance has not grown over the past few decades. A study by Duke University noted that "most congregations in the United States are small, but most people are in large congregations." According to the study, the average congregation had just seventy-five regular participants, while the average church attendee worshiped in a gathering with about four hundred weekly participants.[3]

For the past thirty years or so, many churches have sought to be "seeker friendly" or "seeker sensitive" as a way of marketing and packaging the church. This movement took off in the mid-'90s as the Los Angeles–area Saddleback Church and Chicago-area Willow Creek megachurches rose to prominence. It's significant that these churches were located in two of the three top labor markets in the United States. Megachurch pastors Robert Schuller of Crystal Cathedral, Bill Hybels of Willow Creek, and Rick Warren of Saddleback Church (and author of *The Purpose Driven Church*, among others) inspired the seeker-sensitive model of ministry. In 2008, *Christianity Today* reported that "since 1975, Willow Creek has avoided conventional church approaches, using its Sunday services to reach the unchurched through polished music, multimedia, and sermons referencing popular culture and other familiar themes. The church's leadership believed the approach would attract people searching for answers, bring them into a relationship with Christ, and then capitalize on their contagious fervor to evangelize others."[4]

The seeker-friendly movement was effective for a time in drawing a large number of people to the faith. But the leaders of Willow Creek admitted in 2008 that although the church had helped many people find new faith in Jesus, they had failed to teach them how to practice the spiritual disciplines needed to grow their faith. This is one reason I emphasize discipleship in this book. We can learn from both the successes and the failures of the megachurches.

The established church often tends to tear apart anything that it does not see as "real evangelism." We cloak our biases, insecurities, and fears in theology, the theology of our limited cultural perspective. We think that an organized, well-thought-out plan somehow lacks spirituality, as if Jesus and the disciples just showed up at locations without some type of advertising or organized logistics, even if they were organized by word of mouth. Jesus was quite the savvy communicator, and he broke a few sacred paradigms as he sat with tax collectors, publicly healed the sick on the Sabbath, and drank water from a Samaritan woman. The church can be a tad self-righteous and envious when others are reaching people that we can't. Small church leaders condemn megachurches for being too popular. Megachurches often try to out "mega" each other, even though Scripture teaches us in Luke 10:2, "He said to them, 'The harvest is plentiful, but the laborers are few; therefore ask the Lord of the harvest to send out laborers into his harvest.'" Again, this is not about congregational size. We must activate for spiritual growth and community engagement.

Reflecting on my conversation with Alex, I thought about the technology and other online applications I used to connect with people during my days as an event planner. I planned city-wide religious conferences for the denomination for which I worked. Sunday service and other congregational gatherings are spiritually focused events. Why not modernize how we engage and connect with people? The Internet, the smartphone, and other advances, if used effectively, help us reach more people and share information with people more efficiently.

Technology and other practical advances have always shaped the church, often in great and powerful ways. In the mid-1450s, inventor Johannes Gutenberg, printer Peter Schöffer, and financier Johann Fürst collaborated to publish a Bible. The printed Bible "posed a fundamental challenge to papal dominion," writes scholar Justin Champion. "Cheap Bibles meant more readers and, ultimately, more debate over the meaning of God's word. While the Gutenberg Bible was primarily for elite clerical usage, it opened the door to mass and untutored readings and interpretations. The ability to produce hundreds, if not tens of thousands, of copies made the Bible a commercial opportunity and a cultural revolution."[5] The Gutenberg Bible might have been the originating spark of the seeker-friendly movement.

Believe it or not, there are ways to do pastoral care, Bible study, and worship virtually. Since I began writing this book, pretty much every church in America has shifted to some type of digital engagement because of the COVID-19 pandemic. (Apparently, I knew what I was talking about; now, I just need to work on my timing and learning when to invest in webcams and online streaming services. Both yeast and webcams disappeared in 2020, to the chagrin of pastors and hospitality committee members everywhere.) Before the pandemic began, I wrote that the contemporary church needs to seriously consider creating digital connections to foster spiritual relationships. Post COVID-19, this will no longer be optional for many churches. It will be a necessity if they want to be a part of the lasting change discussed in this book. Larger seeker-friendly churches and churches with younger leadership are finding ways to create a robust ministerial culture using video streaming and other online tools.

Digital natives, such as millennials and members of Gen Z, value online interactions as much as they do in-person relationships. Their connection to their virtual relationship runs pretty deep. Thanks in large part to the 2020 coronavirus pandemic, many of us, even Gen Xers and baby boomers, have fully embraced online community. Physical church versus online church is no longer an either-or proposition. It is now a both-and necessity for the active church. Streaming is also a way to bring cohesion across multiple campuses and smaller community groups. One added benefit of online church is the ability to use analytical tools to monitor engagement and reach. Data is a good thing. In the past, we got our data from the usher headcount or the treasurer's report. Now we can download data. If we have the right team and software, we can get more beneficial information about our congregation members and their spiritual needs than we could ever get from traditional surveys and assessment methods. There are so many ways for the savvy, seeker-optimized organization to transform its digital connections into real-life communities, where online viewers can join a physical campus and enjoy their worship experience surrounded by peers.

The primary complaints I hear about the seeker-sensitive movement are the following:

1. It turns people into casual consumers of the gospel.

2. It minimizes the emphasis on truth and is too focused on not offending people.

3. It focuses on services and church programs built around "meeting people's felt needs" as the end goal.

If we measure church success by the size of the building, the size of the membership roll, or the size of the offering, we are missing what it means to be an activated church. We should keep the following concepts in mind:

1. *The church must attract people at all levels of commitment.* Not everyone is going to be as committed as the apostles—and when the going got tough, even the apostle Peter denied his relationship with Christ. Are we communicating that everyone attending our church needs a degree in theology or needs to have a deep understanding of atonement theory to be a part of our body? We need to engage people where they are at and not let our theological arrogance mimic that of those opposed

to putting cheap printed Bibles in the hands of the unwashed masses. Can you even imagine saying that today? I genuinely don't see a problem with having "open house" type services to introduce people to the gospel and the weirdness of church culture in an appealing manner. But there should also be other programs for the more seasoned and knowledgeable saints. I have been to too many churches where I wanted to run out after my first few minutes in the building. One congregation was so "high church" that all the robes, crosses, and church-speak made me feel that I was going to mess up something. One congregation was so "low church" that I wondered if I was at a private party. People were barefoot, eating breakfast tacos, and pretty much ignoring me. I am a church professional, and I felt lost. How do we attract the unchurched?

2. *While our goal is not to water down the gospel, our goal should not be to be offensive, either.* The extreme of never talking about sin or the hard stuff of the Bible should not be counterbalanced by always talking about sin and the hard stuff of the Bible. Scripture also reminds of the need to nurture spiritual growth and maturity. People learn and understand at differing levels, and we also respond to different stimuli that spark spiritual transformation. "For though by this time you ought to be teachers, you need someone to teach you again the basic elements of the oracles of God. You need milk, not solid food; for everyone who lives on milk, being still an infant, is unskilled in the word of righteousness. But solid food is for the mature, for those whose faculties have been trained by practice to distinguish good from evil" (Hebrews 5:12-14). The gospel is not one-size-fits-all, even though it is one gospel. Jesus spoke the appropriate word to the proper people, and his harshest criticism was not for the woman accused of adultery but for religious leaders more concerned with the letter of the law than with the Spirit of God.

When I was a cadet at the United States Air Force Academy, I was forced to memorize Major General John M. Schofield's address to the Corps of Cadets, U.S. Military Academy, in August 1879.

The discipline which makes the soldiers of a free country reliable in battle is not to be gained by harsh or tyrannical treatment. On the contrary, such treatment is far more likely to destroy than to make an army. It is possible to impart instruction and to give commands in such a manner and such a tone of voice to inspire in the soldier no feeling but an intense desire to obey, while the opposite manner and tone of voice cannot fail to excite strong resentment and a desire to disobey. The one mode or the other of dealing with subordinates springs from a corresponding spirit in the breast of the commander. He who feels the respect which is due to others cannot fail to inspire in them regard for himself, while he who feels, and hence manifests, disrespect toward others, especially his inferiors, cannot fail to inspire hatred against himself.

Although I now lead a historic peace church, this message from a military leader is always in the forefront of my mind as I think about compassionate leadership. I have seen peace church leaders treat people horribly. How is it that a man like Schofield, sending people to die in war, is more compassionate than leaders trying to lead people to everlasting life? We can't extend less grace and love than God has extended to us (Ephesians 2:1-10).

3. *If we are not designing programs and services around the needs of the people, for whom are they developed?* This criticism of the seeker movement smacks of institutional arrogance. The growth of the early church was, in large part, related to its communication to the community. "All who believed were together and had all things in common; they would sell their possessions

and goods and distribute the proceeds to all, as any had need. Day by day, as they spent much time together in the temple, they broke bread at home and ate their food with glad and generous hearts, praising God and having the goodwill of all the people. And day by day the Lord added to their number those who were being saved" (Acts 2:44-47). People were saved, and the church grew because the church catered to the people and their needs—spiritual, financial, physical, and emotional.

I asked Pastor Misha, who leads a congregation of about seventy people, for her thoughts on church growth. She responded, "The church has grown despite my best efforts."

Puzzled, I asked, "You don't want the church to grow?"

She replied, "You know, I'm not invested in that. I think I've been a little wary of the seeker-friendly movement. Sometimes church needs to be hard, and that is okay. People need to invest in the movement. The church is not about whatever works for you. I want people to encounter Jesus. That is sometimes a lot. I don't want to downplay what that means when people come to my church. People should think, 'What does it mean to actually follow Jesus? What might following Jesus mean for us?' And it's not always hard, but it does mean making some cultural shifts."

I agree with Pastor Misha that numerical growth is not as significant as spiritual growth, but I was intrigued by her statement "The church has grown despite my best efforts." While she does not embrace the seeker-friendly movement, she is very active in the community and on social media. In fact, her social media skills are way above average, if not prolific. She has a distinct ministry focus, and she knows how to use her online presence as an extension of the ministry in which she is engaging. Her goal is not to build a large congregation, but she is intentional about fostering growth and spiritual movement.

Pastor Misha went on to express the need for deep relationships in a church. "We make decisions together. We work on building consensus on important matters. That's a tough thing for people to figure out. We must be able to hear each other deeply and trust each other. If you want to be part of it, that's great, but you have to know everybody. You have to have consistent relationships to be able to come to a consensus. You really have to care about each other and listen to each other. You can't just show up on Sundays and expect that to happen. Those types of bonds need to be cultivated in the congregation."

One thing the activated church does not do is chase fads, fame, or fortune. Membership success is not a measure of community significance. Significance comes from having a transformational impact on the lives of others. Membership success amplifies the message "Look at me, look how many folks I can fit in this room once a month." I spent seventeen years in congregational ministry, followed by ten years in denominational leadership, so I understand the economics of running a ministry very well. Often, having more members translates to more money and a bigger budget to enhance programming and staff time. But the goal of the church is not to be the biggest or shiniest option for belonging. NFL games and blockbuster movies draw big crowds, but they don't bring lasting change in the lives of participants. For churches, the goal should be becoming competent in the mission of transformation.

Rather than seeker-friendly churches, we need "SEO savvy" congregations and leaders who can leverage the digital and the physical witness to connect, unite, and mobilize people for ministry. SEO stands for *search engine optimization*, a term for digital marketing practices that increase the quantity and quality of Internet traffic to a website or other resource. In our contemporary context, being able to engage people online is as vital as the apostle Paul's ability to write. People should be able to easily find us and the services that we offer. And we must witness to people in the places where they reside and work. For people born into Gen X or younger, that place includes the Internet. People who are part of Generation Z are digital natives with whom it is almost impossible for a church to connect unless it is SEO savvy. Not every pastor must be a technology expert, but churches cannot ignore the impact of the online landscape any more than they can ignore the physical landscape of the communities in which they exist.

A better definition for an "SEO savvy" church might be a *seeker-engaging organization*. While engaging with people who are seeking a congregation in the digital realm is crucial, doing so in the physical realm is equally important. The goal of bringing people together in the church environment is not simply to be friendly. We want to engage people where they are in their lives, and we want to build an organizational structure around them that allows them to grow and thrive spiritually.

Several factors come into play as you go through a seeker-engaging organizational process. I believe these factors are consistent with the gospel and necessary for the church of today to be relevant. Here are a few things to think about when you are looking at SEO as it applies to ministry:

1. *Know your audience or your community.* Whom are you reaching and whom do you want to reach?
2. *Where do you rank amid other congregations in your community?* The critical question is, "What makes you stand out as a church?" The answer can be something as simple as "We preach the gospel." But I would counter, "Are you the only church that preaches the gospel, and what does that mean exactly?" There must be clarity in the message that we share as ministries—more of that in the chapter on identity. Maybe you are the only church in town, and that can be an essential reason

for you to exist. I go to some cities, and there are seemingly fifteen churches within a square mile of each other. And some of those churches are crumbling effigies of a time gone by. Clearly, they don't all have an essential reason to exist.

3. *Engagement experience.* In the digital marketing industry, you want your clients and visitors to have a positive first experience. You also want your website to be easy to navigate. Those are valuable lessons for the church. When people come into our doors, we want them to interact. We want them to engage with the life and programs of the congregation. We recognize first-time visitors and we offer special parking spots. We want people to pray; we want people to share information. Many churches actively feed the hungry and care for the sick. All of these things are interactions, engagements—not too different from what we do on social media and other online platforms. To be an effective ministry, we must understand both the physical and the digital space in which people interact. Online and in physical areas, we can worship, share concerns, and pray with one another. For those who think this goes too far, I need only point out the use of the telephone or written prayer chains. Those are the technologies that churches adopted in the past to create better engagement. The internet is now a more efficient way to share today's prayer chain or to set up today's prayer hotline.

4. *Who is engaging?* We need to know who is coming to our churches, why they're coming, and if they are staying. If they aren't staying, we need to understand why. I do think churches must understand who they are and why they exist; coupling the reason with the clear understanding that we can't be all things to all people. Churches need to ask themselves if they are reaching the people whom they desire to reach. And if they aren't reaching the people they think they should reach, they need to understand the barriers.

5. *Create funnels for increased engagement.* "Click funnels" are one of the techniques used by web-based marketing companies. The goal is to get website users to click on certain things until they go deeper and deeper and engage more and more with the site's content. Typically, the site designer wants the user to buy a product. So they offer users some free things or some surface-level items to get them to make the big purchase. I do think that this principle applies to the church. As Christians, the goal is to draw people into the body and, hopefully, to get them to commit to a deeper and deeper relationship with Christ. I know the marketing terms sometimes turn us off, but the church should be leaders when we think about engaging people and fostering deep relationships. While the marketing industry may want you to give up more of your money and data, the church wants you to give up everything and be committed to Christ.

6. *Analytics.* Google is the king of analytics when it comes to search engine optimization, but the church also needs data. When I was coming up, the ushers would walk around with a clicker or a tally sheet to figure out how many people were in attendance at church. The trustees used a calculator and a ledger to keep track of finances. We depended on the elders and deacons of the church to keep a watchful eye out for missing members. Embracing systems and technology will allow us to do better. By using the tools of today, we can get a better sense of how well our programs are working. The right tools will also help us be better stewards of congregant-donated resources. The church should not be so data-driven that it forgets the human and spiritual aspect of its being, but the church needs information. The church needs accurate records for accountability and to measure growth and transformation.

Even as we embrace technology and different strategies, leadership is the most crucial aspect of a fruitful ministry. I like to say that leadership is everything. Now, leadership is not the only thing, but leadership is essential. I'm not saying that the church should wrap itself up in the personality of one person. I'm not in favor of setting up iconic leaders, but whatever type of leadership structure your church chooses to have, it needs to work. Too many religious leadership structures are a hot mess of bureaucracy. No one knows who is in charge. There is no clarity on how decisions get made. In fact, systems have sometimes been designed out of fear of strong leadership. These layered fear-based systems, in my experience, lead to abuse and corruption. I do observe that throughout the Bible, God has worked through strong leaders of differing capacities. Often, these influential leaders came from outside the predictable establishment mold, but that is another book. The activated church needs transparent transformational leadership. There are far too many pastors and church boards filled with managers trying to hold on to the status quo. I will dive deeper into leadership later in the book.

Transformation is an operation of change. Before you continue reading this book, I want to warn you. Change is difficult. Change can be upsetting. Change can be a risky undertaking; lasting successful change has a distinct, methodical pace. If you are looking for a quick fix to your ministry or if you are not willing to do the hard work to transform your congregation and your community, throw this book away and take comfort in your old traditions. Don't rock the boat. This book is for leaders who are willing to risk sinking, like the apostle Peter boldly stepping out of the boat, in order to answer the call of Christ in their community. Don't read this book if you want to do church as usual or if you are interested in doing a safe "country club" or "members only" church.

The church needs to change if it wants to remain relevant and if it wants to live into the great commission.

Here is the pushback you may receive as you try to implement the strategies in this book:

1. You are trying to run the church like a business.
2. We need to focus on getting people into the church (the building).
3. This businesslike approach doesn't feed people's souls.
4. The tools are too narrowly focused.
5. It is tough on the staff and volunteers.
6. It's not biblical.
7. It won't work.

Maybe we did not grasp the depth and commitment needed to pull off the seeker movement. Organizations can drift from good foundations. Yes, Willow Creek acknowledged that it needed to make some leadership and operational changes. Too often, we try to emulate the success of others, looking for a magic potion or that secret sauce. As I have watched gurus and masters try to teach about their success, I have often found they leave out many details. Yes, the secret sauce recipe often lists the ingredients, but it fails to detail the preparation, the hard work, and the grinding needed to pull it off. The secret isn't in the sauce so much as it is in the mixing, the measuring, and the tiny adjustments that form the ingredients into something great. It is the small tasks performed over and over that help us achieve our goals. Ministry is no different.

When I began writing this section of the book, I was a little concerned that it would come across as too modern, too techy. I talked a lot about SEO, which I renamed as seeker-engaging organization. The chaos of the global coronavirus pandemic of 2020 has revealed the benefits of technology. Many churches faced a great deal of uncertainty about how they were going to connect with members because many cities and states across the country issued orders minimizing the number of people that could gather. It simply was not safe for church members to gather in the traditional manner. Churches were scrambling, trying to figure out how to do effective ministry online, and how to connect with members during this crisis. Many had no way to receive tithes and offerings online, or at least they had not developed doing so as a cultural practice. Some churches were prepared because they had established an online presence in addition to their physical campus. For example, I have always been somewhat of a tech geek. I had an inhouse studio ready to go and all the systems I need to connect with my staff and pastors across the country. It wasn't hard for my team and me to pivot, because we had already been gearing up for the digital sphere.

I guarantee that all the tools and tips that I share in this book will lead to success if you are willing to grind through them intentionally, and if you have faith. There is no magic potion; there is no secret sauce; there is just great execution built on a strong foundation. Preparation pays off, and God gives us the increase. Let's start thinking beyond how we traditionally do church and find new models to engage the new generation.

QUESTIONS FOR REFLECTION

1. What valuable information do you track regarding your members and their engagement?

2. How well are you able to communicate with your members during times of crisis?

3. How often do you review and test your crisis management plans?

4. Do you have a robust online presence? What are the gaps?

5. How well do you integrate your online program with your physical program? Do these programs enhance each other?

6. What lessons did your congregation learn during the COVID-19 pandemic that still need to be implemented as you move forward?

7. Where does your ministry rank in online searches?

THREE

Characteristic One:
Know Your Identity; Show Your Identity

According to the grace of God given to me, like a skilled master builder I laid a foundation, and someone else is building on it. Each builder must choose with care how to build on it.

—1 CORINTHIANS 3:10

IMAGINE THAT YOU are walking down the street in Anywhere, USA. Pat from Pasadena stops you and says, "Hey, I am new in town. I'm looking for a church. Tell me what is special about your church." How would you respond? What is so special about your congregation that it even needs to exist? What is the niche that you fill in your community?

The activated church has a clear sense of its identity in the community. If Pat from Pasadena were to ask a member of an activated church, "What is special about your church?" the member would have an answer. Depending on the congregation, the response may sound a bit like this:

- We serve the homeless and immigrant populations by partnering with the city and other local congregations.

- We have a phenomenal ministry to families with school-age children. We are very much engaged with the local schools.

- We have a healing ministry. We believe in the power of prayer to make a difference in our community. We pray for anybody, anywhere, at any time. Can I pray for you?

- We serve the religious, academic community. Many seminarians and scholars come to our church. If you like hermeneutics, come to our church. We believe in equipping through education.

- We are called to transform lives, restore hope, and build community. Why don't you come for a visit or watch us online?

- We are focused on transformation through social justice and reconciliation. Our church is welcoming to all.

- We have the best potlucks and cornhole tournaments.

These are just a few examples of ways that congregations might express their identity through active engagement of their community. I am not sure that either cornhole or hermeneutics are the best selling points for me, but depending on the community, those might be areas of need. (Okay, I don't actually know any activated churches that are using cornhole and potlucks as effective discipleship tools, so hopefully that would not be what we tell Pat from Pasadena.) The thriving church must know its primary mission and the vision God has given it for the community.

To thrive, congregations and congregational leaders must have a keen understanding of who they are in relation to the culture, their context, and the call of God, but must do so without succumbing to the surrounding culture, as Israel did in the book of Hosea. As my former pastor used to say, "You have to know who you are and whose you are [if you want to be an effective Christian leader]." In other words, your leadership should be rooted in Christ, and you need a depth of understanding of the gifts God has given you.

Churches are not exempt from the culture wars that are going on in the rest of society. Congregational leaders will always be pulled by the polarization and politics of society. Segments of the church in America have always struggled with the issue of identity, often lagging behind the pace of societal change. One example of this can be seen in the way that the church in America related to systemic racial inequity. Starting around the eighteenth century and stretching into the twentieth, when the Civil Rights Act of 1964 outlawed discrimination on the basis of race, color, and several other factors, many evangelicals used religion to justify slavery and segregation. As a result, the church was not a place of liberation, but one of subjugation for many. This subjugation can be seen in the baptismal vows for slaves written by French missionary Francis Le Jau, which read, "You declare in the presence of God and before this congregation that you do not ask for holy baptism out of any design to free yourself from the Duty and Obedience you owe to your Master while you live, but merely for the good of your soul."[1] At the same time, others in the church rejected the evils of slavery and racial segregation and pushed for reform. Over time, the church has shifted, and must continue to shift in similar ways in response to the awakenings in our broader culture to remain relevant and responsive to the Spirit.

Our identity is the blueprint of the vision. A strong vision does one primary thing for a congregation: it creates clarity. Clarity creates movement in the local church. The authors of *Simple Church* put it this way: "Clarity is the ability of the process to be communicated and understood by the people. You are a builder, and it is time to design a ministry blueprint."[2] Your ministry blueprint or identity starts with the following:

- Understanding your unique giftings.

- Knowing the community to which you are called.

- Having a strong sense of the type of disciples you want to create.

- Having a sense of the transformation you want to see manifested in the lives of people.

The activated church has a vision that allows it to see beyond the present circumstances. The vision, the strong sense of identity, and the revealing of self-awareness pulls the activated church to a place of life. Congregations and congregational leaders without this strong sense of identity often find themselves in turmoil or fading from existence. We have to know our identity, and we have to demonstrate or live into that identity as we serve the community. The church needs to create a culture of people who buy into the vision.

Where there is no revelation [or vision], the people cast off restraint. (Proverbs 29:18 NKJV)

My people are destroyed for lack of knowledge. (Hosea 4:6)

Without a clear vision and an articulable blueprint for the ministry, it is easier to get distracted and drawn in any number of directions. Imagine if a builder poured the foundation for a building without a good blueprint for the rest of the structure. Imagine what a mess it would be when it came time to frame the house. Better yet, imagine if the construction crew had one set of blueprints, the plumber another set, and the electrician a third. The final monstrosity, if it were ever built, would be a nonfunctional and possibly unsafe mess.

I have been to towns that, as my daughter would say, "literally" have a church building every quarter of a mile. Many of the churches are small. Some are struggling to find pastors, in addition to finding people to hear their preaching. Why are there so many churches in one location? Are the needs of this community that great, or is there so much division in the Christian world that we cannot work together to build fewer, stronger congregations? Ministry can be hard work. It's even tougher with limited financial and people resources. It is particularly difficult when congregations are stepping on one another's toes and duplicating the same services while ignoring other needs in the community that are falling through the gaps.

First Chronicles 12:32 illustrates the impact that wisdom has over brute force and power. When facing a war, David singled out two hundred unarmed leaders of the tribe of Issachar, along with their relatives, from the rest of his army. This small group of people understood the signs of the times and knew the best course for Israel to take. They are mentioned not because of their ability to fight, but because of their understanding of context. Living into your identity, while strategic, isn't necessarily about brute force. I do not believe leaders or congregations should "fake the funk"—an idiom that means to perform outside the range of one's capabilities. The sons of Issachar had unique gifts that stood out. The activated church must always ask who we are, and how God is calling us to respond. Church leadership teams need to consider their collective gifts and experience and how they will use those to shape their ministry.

UNDERSTAND YOUR UNIQUE GIFTS

Developing a sense of vision is an underrated leadership skill. All great leaders have a great vision rooted in a deep understanding of their identity. Understanding who God has designed you to be and then doing your best to live into that design brings a sense of peace.

The story of Moses is an excellent example to highlight that, while chance and circumstance can influence our identity, it is still up to us to live into that identity. I've intentionally labeled this "chance and circumstance" rather than "destiny" or "misfortune." I avoid the term *destiny* because the modern usage of the word makes it appear that we play no active role in our success or failures. Some people believe in predestination. People often say, "Well, this is the life God planned for me." If I have learned anything in life, it is to "never get involved in a land war in Asia" (google that phrase along with "*The Princess Bride*" and thank me later) and to never argue about destiny with a Calvinist. So, if you are a Calvinist, just skip the next paragraph; you might not like what I am going to say.

I believe God gives us a choice. Moses chose to lead the children of Israel. He drew on all his experiences and the clash of cultures that was his life to solidify his identity as one of the greatest prophets ever. Can you imagine the identity conflict with which he had to wrestle? "Do I hang with the Hebrew side of my family and this bush, or do I go with rich Grandpa Pharaoh?"

We may have all the opportunities in the world thrown at us, but that will not make us successful. While we may seem to have a preordained path in life, we still must choose to walk down that path to get to where God wants us. The GPS in a car can give us turn-by-turn navigation, but how many of us ignore it because we know a shortcut? *We often think people achieve success through dumb luck, but luck is the place where opportunity and preparation converge.* I'm not advocating playing the lottery, but heck, even if you win the lottery, someone had to go to the store and purchase the ticket. The luck fairy does not just leave winning lotto tickets under your pillow.

Moses was uniquely positioned to serve as the channel between God and the Hebrews and to broker their freedom from Egypt. He was the child of two cultures. While the Bible doesn't speak much about Moses's years growing up in the Egyptian court, one must assume that as a child of the pharaoh's daughter, he had instruction in religious, civil, and military matters. Since Egypt controlled Canaan and part of Syria and had connections with other nations of the Fertile Crescent, Moses undoubtedly had a general knowledge of life in the ancient Near East. This education in leadership, combined with his dual ethnic identity, made him the best person to serve as a conduit to freedom. Moses was a soldier and logistical leader who brought together two cultures, but he also was in tune with who he was not. He lacked the confidence and skill to be the spokesperson for his people. The boy drawn from the water also probably lacked the temperament to be a high priest; to compensate, he brought in his brother Aaron to fill the gaps.

As we think about spiritual gifts in the church, we normally just look to the fivefold ministry model listed in Ephesians: apostle, prophet, evangelist, pastor, and teacher. First Corinthians 12:8-10 adds the ministries of miracles, helps, healing, and administration. Stop reading for a few minutes, set this book aside, and reflect on your unique gifts combined with the positions in which you serve. I like to think of the list in Ephesians as job titles, and that the list in Corinthians adds some preferred skills to go along with the role. Think about it. Moses was a prophet (title). But he also performed a bunch of miracles (skill). Aaron, his brother, was a pastor/priest (title), but he was good with administration (skill).

As a youth pastor, I brought several unique skills to my role. I am a great administrator and I plan fantastic, fun events (on top of that I am extremely humble!). Those skills became a big part of my youth ministry. Using these skills, I created an event called Club Chosen, which drew teens from around the city. We had disco lights, a Christian DJ, non-alcoholic fruity beverages with umbrellas and whipped cream. I threw some of the best Christian teen parties and gatherings in the city. Those events drew in kids. I provided an alternative, safe place for kids to come to on Friday nights. It kept the kids of my city out of trouble, exposed them to church, and opened the door for discipleship opportunities. That worked for me, and it worked for the needs of the community (I even got a grant from the city for my first event). In the early 2000s, it also worked for my millennial youth, before they were so named. Our youth ministry didn't ignore traditional Bible study and prayer. We had that too. But I knew I connected with a certain type of kid with certain needs, and I did not run from that primary audience. The core youth I was most effective with was drawn to my "style." Like Moses, I surrounded myself with the right leaders who brought other gifts, and we worked together to increase the appeal of the ministry while shining light on the blind spots. The ministry was still greatly influenced by my gifts, which is appropriate. Activated church leaders have to be comfortable with and appropriately manage the influence that results from the leadership gifts they have.

As a youth pastor, I was approached by many well-meaning parents who gave me suggestions for the programming I should provide for their children. Some of their suggestions included taking students on tours of colleges, starting a basketball team, providing financial counseling, offering etiquette classes, and holding Christian proms. There were many good ideas, but I knew the ministry to which I was called and the focus of youth programming for our church. We had specific goals for the impact we wanted to have in the lives of the youth at our church, so we focused primarily on activities that drew on the unique skill set of our staff and the resources we had available, and that would contribute to what we hoped to accomplish in the community.

Does that mean we rejected good suggestions? No, we did one of three things when people brought us suggestions:

1. We referred parents to other organizations in the community who specialized in the area of ministry we could not provide.

2. We partnered with others to increase our capacity.

3. We clearly articulated that the suggested ministry was not in our wheelhouse.

Sometimes I would challenge the person who was passionate about what I was doing to develop a program themselves and bring it back to me; 99 percent of the time, I never heard from that person again. But sometimes, rarely, I would gain a new powerful leader. That person contributed an idea that was in line with the goals of the ministry, and they were willing to get their hands dirty, contributing to the outcome. Having people catch the vision and pour themselves into it is one of the advantages of understanding your identity and communicating it with clarity.

Identity in the activated church is an intersection of many personal identities coming together. It is shaped by the individuals of the leadership team, the community, and the congregation. While I believe in adaptability, for those in positions of primary leadership, we want to make sure our leadership gifts line up with the needs of the community. Sometimes our gifts are not the right fit, and trying to brute-force an alignment puts our ministry into an unhealthy place. I am fortunate that the roles in which I have served fit my style. I would not have accepted a position in a ministry role that was at odds with my gifting or that was not willing to shift appropriately. One of my favorite lines of dialogue comes from the 2001 film *Along Came a Spider* (based on the book by James Patterson). It is a powerful reminder to us as individual leaders and to the institutions to which we belong to commit to our calling. The scene between Alex Cross and Jezzie Flanigan goes like this:

Alex: You do what you are, Jezzie.

Jezzie: You mean, you are what you do.

Alex: No, I mean you do what you are. You're born with a gift. If not that, then you get good at something along the way. And what you're good at, you don't take for granted. You don't betray it.

Jezzie: What if you do betray your gift?

Alex: Then, you betray yourself. That's a sad thing.

Know your call. Don't betray your call. Hopefully, part of the reason both the leader and the congregation are serving in a specific community is that there is a good fit between the three entities (leadership, congregation, and community). I am a firm believer that congregations need to look like the communities to which they belong. If they do not, something is out of place. The congregation that cuts itself off from the heartbeat of the community will eventually wither and die. I have seen too many empty shells, buildings that were once vibrant churches before something happened. The neighborhood changed, peo-

ple moved on, but the church and leadership remained stead-
fast and immovable. The congregants eventually got older and
older and eventually grayed themselves out of relevancy, and
only the shell of a church remained.

One Methodist church in Minnesota decided it would fight
this trend of death by graying membership by revitalizing its
congregation and reconnecting with the community. When
Grove United Methodist Church in Cottage Grove, a sub-
urb of St. Paul, recognized that it needed a revitalization, the
church asked older parishioners to leave for a time so that the
church could attract younger families. A church leader noted,
"The campus has struggled to attract new members, particularly younger people, despite Cottage Grove existing as one of the
fastest-growing cities in Minnesota." The decision was controversial enough that it made national news, and many people
were outraged. The reporting made it sound like church leaders
were ejecting elderly members out on the street, but that was
not the case. According to Dan Wetterstrom, the lead pastor of
Grove United, the revitalized Cottage Grove campus would be
inclusive and open to "anyone and everyone who wants to be
a part of it." As CNN reported, "church leaders have a specific
mission in mind, and they want the new community to consist
of those who feel a calling to do that work. Because of that,
[Wetterstrom] said the new community might not be the best
fit for everyone."[3]

Wetterstrom repeated the theme named by many of the people I interviewed for this book. He lifted up discipleship and
transformation as critical reasons for the revitalization efforts
of the church. I appreciate that this congregation realized there
was a gap between their identity and that of the surrounding
community. In a fast-growing part of the community, the congregation was not thriving. Without radical change, it could
not draw in the people from the new community demographic.

We must understand who we are and that we may appeal to different people at different times in their walk of faith. We aren't equipped to be all things to all people. The church that understands its identity can then create essential partnerships throughout the community to ensure that the needs of the members of the community are met. The authors of *Simple Church* point out, "There is an epidemic of fast-food spirituality among believers today. We like big spiritual menus with lots of options. And we want those options served to us fast."[4] To extend this fast-food analogy, I'd encourage us to look at our congregations more as a Five Guys rather than a Golden Corral. In the world of fast food, restaurants like Five Guys have a simple menu with every item freshly made to order. At Five Guys, you can only get a burger or a hotdog, but it's always excellent. At Golden Corral, you can get burgers, steak, a chocolate fountain, fish, Chinese food, pasta, pizza, et cetera, served in mass quantities over steaming water baths. Which is better? When it comes to relevance and serving the community, variety may not be the spice of life. Churches should not be grand buffets that value quantity and variety over quality. Churches should understand their own particular strengths and develop their ministry based on those strengths. Yet we often try to hold on to members who are looking for something other than what we do well and to hold on to positions in the community in which we are ill-equipped to serve.

In the business world, the approach of focusing on doing one thing very well is called niche marketing. Businesses realize that different business sectors usually have different target markets, and different strengths are needed to be competitive and profitable in each of these markets. Focusing on one niche market is usually a much better business strategy than splitting a business's resources among several. "Where a business is dominant in its narrowly defined niche, it is likely to make several times the returns where one faces a dominant competitor (the mirror image)," writes entrepreneur Richard Koch.[5] Businesses understand that simplicity wins and that complexity costs. If profit-driven organizations understand this, why can't the nonprofit church understand it? It boggles my mind. I have served under all types of church structures: pastor-controlled, elder-controlled, congregational polity, deacon-controlled, and a mishmash of styles. Two things are true in my experience: (1) corruption can occur under any leadership model, and (2) a strong vision covers a multitude of leadership sins.

Again, vision begets clarity by empowering folks to know what they are supposed to do. They are not waiting on the bureaucracy to prompt them to act. Part of the problem with church leadership is "The Lord." Please don't think I am a heretic, but it seems that for some reason, those who quote "The Lord" and those who argue that "we prayed about it" can never get their stories straight with each other. I would bet that those phrases pop up in many a bad church business meeting, creating division wrapped in spiritual mumbo jumbo. I cannot help but call it false spirituality, and it is a plague to the church and true spiritual discernment. This false "discerning" ear is another example of why it's important to have a vision and the blueprint identity for your ministry. When those who claim authority from "The Lord" and because "we prayed about it" want to shift the conversation, you will have done spiritual discernment in advance to guide your response. At that point, you just need to ask, "Does this fit into who we are and how we do things?" Hopefully, this piece of advice cuts down on the number of meetings you need to have and divisions in the church. If I am honest, sometimes I just say, "Well, the Lord didn't tell me that," and I move on. I have been around too long to waste time with nonsense. But I would suggest that you try the thoughtful approach, especially if you are a young leader who may still be establishing a leadership identity.

Knowing your identity and avoiding distractions will save you time, money, and other valuable resources. Typically, churches have fewer resources than for-profit companies, and our resources are donated by our members. If any organization understands the cost of complexity, the church should. We have an obligation to be good stewards of the donations we receive. But the nonactivated church tries to be the community buffet, trying to please everyone and answer every need, rather than operate within a focused call. Too many churches operate with the mentality of "more is better." We try to outshine each other and to replicate program after program instead of partnering with each other to serve the community. For those concerned about diversity or reaching more marginalized groups, I address those topics in the chapter on developing strategic partnerships.

Since the church is not for profit, we don't seek to "dominate" markets, but we must be good stewards, and we want to be facilitators of transformation and healing in the communities we serve. As Jesus told his disciples, "I have told you all this so that you may have peace in me. Here on earth you will have many trials and sorrows. But take heart, because I have overcome the world" (John 16:33 NLT). Churches and other institutions need to have a clear mission and vision. Most often, those are written statements that take a lot of planning and thought, then they get stuck in a drawer somewhere. But that clear articulation of our identity should always be in front of us. It is the lesson of Habakkuk 2:2, and it is the written identity that "runs" the church and its programming decisions. It is a foundation, or blueprint, from 1 Corinthians 3:10 that gives us both the wisdom and the strength to say no when people try to distract us from our calling. With a clear identity that is rooted in our divine call and the needs of the community, we get closer to the people we serve. Instead of becoming an organization of lack, struggling to pay bills and staff, we become an entrenched and essential part of the work of God. We become an activated, thriving church.

HAVE A STRONG SENSE OF THE TYPE OF DISCIPLES YOU WANT TO CREATE

I will talk more about discipleship later in this book. But as we think about creating our identity as a ministry, we need to think about the type of disciples we want to create. The Bible tells us to make disciples, but without the context of Jesus' life, we wouldn't exactly know details about the type of disciples Jesus meant in Matthew 28. So let us think about discipleship, using an analogy that was part of the lifestyle of Jesus and his disciples—fishing. Those of you who are theologians, please bear with me. I am going to shelve the dark judgment motif found in the Old Testament fishing examples of Habakkuk, Jeremiah, and Ezekiel. (I am also very intrigued by the healing passage of Ezekiel 47. Maybe the activated church needs to connect in more prophetic ways when it comes to confronting injustice and creating disciples who are willing to confront it head-on. But I will use the more common interpretation of Matthew 4:19 because many of my readers are familiar with it.)

Let's pretend that I am enjoying pancakes, grits, and bacon on Saturday morning while talking hermeneutics with my new friend, Pat from Pasadena, and watching major league fishing (yes, that is a real thing) on ESPN. There are many different types of fish in the ocean. The tools and techniques that we use to catch a largemouth bass may be different from the tools that we would use to catch a catfish or a saltwater marlin. I'm no fisherman, but as I've watched weekend sports shows, I've concluded that a lot of thought goes into what type of bait and float or lure to use. Depending on what type of fish they are trying to catch, the fishers know what type of item to pull out of the tackle box. And after they catch the fish, the pros have special places to store the fish until they get back to shore.

Just like professional fishers, churches need to know whom they are best equipped to attract and what they're going to do once people become members of the church. What is the desired outcome for new disciples? How will you care for and nurture the folks you catch? Some people catch and release fish so that the fish can go out and create more fish; some people devour every fish they take in; and others catch fish so they can keep them as pets and share their beauty with others. But before you go out and catch fish, you need to know what you're going to do with those fish. (Here we probably should stop the analogy. Don't eat your members or put them in a tank. That would not be good—or legal.)

Churches need to create a road map for people to follow when they become part of a ministry to guide toward the desired end or growth outcome. I am not going to spend too much time on how to do that. Just like weight loss books, there are a hundred books on the journey to church membership and growth groups. I will just offer some advice on logistics. Make joining simple, keep the orientation short, and get the people to engage in serving as soon as possible. Whatever process you choose, your content at a minimum should include the following:

1. Orient people to your congregation and give them a sense of what joining means.

2. Discuss your basic understanding of the Christian faith, what stands out, or what is preeminent for you. New Christians might need additional information, but I see that as a separate process that you set up for new believers versus ministry transplants.

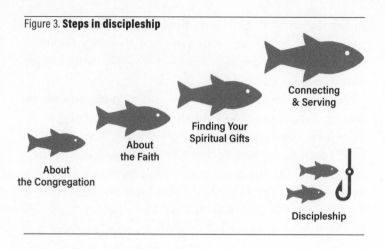

Figure 3. **Steps in discipleship**

3. Help them explore their gifts.

4. Encourage people to serve by presenting them with the opportunities available to them in your congregation.

You can do more, but mapping out and sharing this basic plan will help guide the people you attract. Another important piece of the journey is discipleship. We will dive into that later in the book.

DON'T IGNORE YOUR ONLINE OR YOUR OFFLINE IDENTITY

According to the Pew Research Center, "Young adults are far more likely than older people to have searched online for information about a new congregation. Indeed, 59% of adults under 30 say they have incorporated online searches when looking for a new congregation, compared with just 12% of those ages 65 and older. Still, like their elders, young people are more apt to have attended worship services at congregations they were considering and to have talked with congregation members than they are to have looked for information about congregations online."[6] Having a sharable plan is important.

The same study reports that even 29 percent of nonreligious adults (people who identify as atheists, agnostics, or "nothing in particular" when asked about their religion) have searched for or done some type of research on joining a congregation. So not only is knowing your identity very important to your success, but being able to communicate who you are is also important. People need to know who you are as a church and who they are in relation to membership or involvement.

HAVE A SENSE OF THE TRANSFORMATION YOU WANT TO SEE MANIFESTED IN PEOPLE'S LIVES

Different from discipleship is the transformation you want to see in the lives of people who engage your church. We should think about the transformation that will occur both inside and outside the walls of the church. Will you focus on families, health, economic well-being, or the reduction of violence? I often tell people that serving God should make a difference. I do believe that is true, and hopefully our churches are a part of that process. Jokingly, I sometimes say I have better things to do with my Sundays if coming into church isn't going to affect the way I truly live my life. I know, I know! The really holy people reading this may be appalled. You may be saying, "Glen, it's not all about you." I do understand that, but I wonder what is going through the minds of people who spend their Sundays boating, hanging out at the park, fishing, playing cornhole, or just sleeping late. Why have they prioritized these activities over church attendance? Why isn't the church a bigger draw? When I leave church on Sundays, and people recognize me as a Christian, I want them to notice that something is different about me. When we worship as a body of believers, we give thanks to God by showing our appreciation and adoration. I believe that should also be reflected in how we live our lives. How would a caterpillar feel if after spending all that time inside a cocoon, upon finally breaking free, it didn't have its wings? Our church-es should give our communities wings.

In my role as a denominational leader, I visit lots and lots of churches. I visit churches within my faith tradition, but I also get to visit churches of other faith backgrounds. Sometimes I visit church-in-a-box congregations. These are generic, non-denominational churches that follow specific growth models. They all seem to have the same blueprint. Their physical designs are very similar. They all look like miniature coffee shops; they have the same type of lighting and muted paint. All the pastors wear ripped jeans and Chelsea boots, as if someone is issuing them uniforms. Sometimes I swear I could close my eyes in one city and open my eyes in another, and I wouldn't know that I was at a different church. Of course, these patterns typi-cally appear along certain cultural and theological lines. These churches are run like franchises. If you decide to become a part of a church-in-a-box movement, you will likely have a certain level of success regardless of your location, just like any fran-chise operation such as McDonald's, Burger King, or Dunkin' Donuts. There are some growing church-in-a-box movements, and I am not condemning them. But leaders in these church-in-a-box movements have created blueprints for other leaders to follow that are based on someone else's identity. They are carbon copies of someone else's vision.

There are opportunities for unique ministries to thrive, min-istries that want to reach untapped communities. Not every franchise will work in every community. There are many op-portunities for leaders to reach folks who need specialists and special attention. Ask yourself as a church leader what unique gifts you or your ministry brings. Don't be McDonald's when you can be Chris Madrid's. Chris Madrid's is a forty-four-year-old burger joint in San Antonio, Texas, that serves a tostada burger topped with refried beans and cheese. That probably only works well in San Antonio. Chris Madrid's was devastated by fire in 2017, but the restaurant returned. It is a unique restaurant in the city and is adored by many. It's not just another burger joint. It is part of the community. For eighteen months, customers continued to flock to the business while it was relocated to a food truck. When the restaurant reopened, the owners called on the community to help them decorate the new building to make it feel like home for the people. I doubt the community would have rallied behind a McDonald's or Taco Bell in that way. There is something about a church that has a heart and passion for the community. There is something about a church the serves the spiritual food the community desires and craves. Remember Pat from Pasadena walking down the street in Anywhere, USA? What are you going to serve people like Pat?

Institutions with little sense of identity set themselves up to draw ministry spectators rather than actively engaged members. It is like the story of the little red hen. The little red hen finds a grain of wheat and asks the other farm animals to help her plant it, but they all refuse. At each stage of the process (harvesting, threshing, milling the wheat into flour, and baking the flour into bread), the hen again asks for help from the other animals, but she doesn't receive any help. Finally, after the hen has done all the work, she asks who will help her eat the bread. Of course, this time, everyone eagerly volunteers. But the hen disagrees with them, stating that since no one helped her with her work, no one else would eat the bread. The hen eats it with her chicks, leaving none for anyone else. Ms. Hen, by some standards, was pretty harsh, and some of my more passive church friends might say, "Let's not ruffle feathers; let's share the bread." But this book is for activated church leaders. We cannot be passive about sharing the gospel and discipleship.

As you develop additional programs or evaluate current ones, I want you to focus on providing for those who have decided to wrestle and struggle together as people of faith. I don't want to take the analogy of the little red hen too far, because the church is not in the business of leaving people in need out in the cold. We are called to care for the sick and the widows and to feed the hungry, regardless of whether they contribute to the work of the ministry. I share this story more as a caution against well-meaning members and leaders within the church who have a lot of suggestions that don't line up with the direction in which your individuation congregation has been called.

QUESTIONS FOR REFLECTION

1. Where is complexity costing you?

2. What is your congregation known for in the community? Take the time to ask a few people in the community.

3. What is your stated church mission and vision?

4. Do the answers to questions 1 and 2 match? Why or why not?

5. If you had to start over from scratch, on what ministry services would you focus?

6. Whom do you serve in your church, and do your church membership demographics align with whom you are serving?

FOUR

Characteristic Two:
Mission-Focused Spirituality

> *Therefore confess your sins to one another, and pray for one another, so that you may be healed. The prayer of the righteous is powerful and effective.*
> —JAMES 5:16

EVERY ORGANIZATION NEEDS a clearly defined mission, and the church is no different. The missional church is not a theoretical concept; missions are a necessary tool for the survival of the church. Mission-focused spirituality allows a congregation to see the needs of the community and respond appropriately. In successfully activated churches, mission is manifested both through a relevant word that fits the needs of the people and through corresponding action.

In corporate America, mission is driven by data. Successful corporations measure any number of progress indicators. Corporate organizations are often obsessed with this data, hiring firms to data-mine and track client behavior. Data is useful, and the church needs it too, but we need our faith as well. When the Spirit contradicts data, the activated church is led by the Spirit. An old pastor friend once called the Holy Spirit "the power of God in us, enabling us to have effortless victories." It took me a while to understand what my pastor friend meant. The activated church exercises its faith like a muscle, tapping into the power of the Holy Spirit, so when the time is right—*bam!*—it can effortlessly do the "lifting" that the community needs. Connecting our mission to the Holy Spirit does not mean that we kick back and sip tea while God fixes everything. No, all our hard work comes in the preparation, making the victory or transformation seem effortless to the untrained eye. The Holy Spirit ensures we are ready to fill the needs that the community manifests.

Many of the strategies I share in this book focus on practical and tangible activities. I intentionally interviewed pastors and leaders who possess strong technical skills. This is because of the emphasis of my own training, but also because I find that successful, impactful churches typically have strong technical leadership. But technical skills are not enough, nor do I think they are the most important aspect of church leadership. While it is essential for the church to have strong business practices and well-run organizations, I firmly believe that the power of the church comes from our connection to the Holy Spirit. If we as churches and church leaders aren't tapping into our source, then everything else we do is in vain. Our connection to the Holy Spirit is what allows a church to be more than a social club. I can't emphasize the importance of that distinction enough.

For this chapter, I interviewed a Generation X Hispanic pastor from a large city. His church has a Sunday attendance of fourteen hundred people, and had just completed a building project. Leading a large congregation with a large facility requires impressive technical skills, but I wanted to talk to this pastor about his understanding of the spiritual nature of the church. I asked Pastor Enrique what he thought about running the church like a business as opposed to the spiritual aspects of church leadership. He replied, "While I think it's easy for us to say the church is a business, I think we have to be careful with that. We can't forget that the church is a spiritual organization. We must be in tune with the Spirit. As a pastor, my main goal is to be spiritual, so most of the time, I spend in prayer and Bible study. We also emphasize that with our members. We have teaching series, and we just came out of a twenty-one-day fast. These are activities that we do publicly and unashamedly. Our congregation offers weekly prayer services, and we make sure that prayer and teaching on one's spiritual walk are part of our programming. We are constantly talking about the importance of prayer."

Pastor Enrique went on to say that the spiritual walk of a congregation is what's going to determine the success of the church ultimately. He firmly believes, and I agree, that the church is different from a secular nonprofit. What intrigued me most about our conversation is that Pastor Enrique feels that the spiritual awareness of the church gives us a greater sense of the needs of the community. When the church is in tune with the Holy Spirit and listens to the leading of the Holy Spirit, that allows the church to be more effective in the community. Pastor Enrique described it this way: "You may not be aware of all needs in the community you serve, but being in tune with the spiritual aspect of ministry, walking with God, heightens your senses. It goes beyond the physical question. When you walk up to someone and say, 'Hi, how are you?,' the Spirit may lead you to know that there's something wrong here. I need to pray for the person." He continued, "I've had this experience where I think about somebody, [and] say, 'Hey, why don't you let me pray for you.' And the person responds, 'Wow! You're praying about what I'm going through right now.' The Spirit opens us up to situations that we might otherwise overlook."

For many churches, this balance between spirituality and practicality is a real struggle. On the one hand, we might reject philosophies such as the seeker-friendly movement and being shaped by secular business models. On the other hand, we organize ourselves in a way that leads us to discount the spiritual. We often stifle the leading of the Holy Spirit through our governing practices. There has to be a balance between management practices and tapping into the power of God. Our technical skills need to make room for the Spirit to work.

The biblical story of the feeding of the five thousand illustrates this relationship between spiritual and practical leadership. As we read the biblical story, we tend to focus on the multiplication of the loaves and fish, but I often say the real miracle in this story was in the logistics. I am intrigued with how the disciples got thousands of hungry people to line up in an orderly fashion so that God could bless them.

The story, found in Matthew 14, goes something like this: Jesus was dealing with the death of John the Baptist and had withdrawn, but the crowd found him. Even in his grief, Jesus had compassion on the people, healing the sick and ministering to the masses. The ministry work went on until very late in the day, and Jesus was aware that they would need food, but the crowd wouldn't leave. Because the group was unexpected, there were not enough resources to go around. Jesus gathered the seemingly insufficient supplies that they had, and the Scripture says that he looked to heaven and gave thanks and broke the bread, and then they fed the five thousand men, plus women and children. Miraculously, twelve baskets of broken pieces were left over.

Several things stand out to me in this passage as it relates to mission-based spirituality: First, Jesus was in tune with the needs of the community. He was willing to heal the sick and give a message of hope. But beyond that, he also knew what time the local shops closed, and was considerate enough to try to dismiss the people in time for dinner.

Second, Jesus had help and a plan. It takes a lot to manage and organize over five thousand men, plus the uncounted women and children. Jesus had a team of people who were able to gather resources and help manage this large number of people. I often wonder who was designated to count the men. How in the world would you keep track of that in 30ish AD? Even back then, ushers were obsessed with counting heads!

Third, someone knew where to get enough baskets to hold the upcoming blessings. Good planning and management of resources facilitated the blessing that was about to take place.

Fourth, Jesus had his street team organize the people so that they could receive the blessing.

Finally, the blessing occurred when Jesus looked toward heaven—the source of his power—and prayed over the limited resources. Heaven responded with the resources that the community needed, plus a surplus of twelve baskets of food. Jesus' faith was rewarded, and then some.

When we disconnect the spiritual from the administrative, we fail to understand how these should and can work hand in hand to further the blessings of God and the work that we do in our communities. When it comes to the business of the church, we often check our theology at the boardroom door. We organize with committees and boards, policies, and procedures. We make decisions by voting, relegating prayer to a short devotion or reflection at the beginning of our meetings. I believe that the church works much better when we combine our organizational skills with our skills of praying in faith. The power of prayer and leading by faith cannot be discounted or pushed to the fringes of ministry.

As I mentioned at the beginning of the book, the ability of a congregation to activate a community for meaningful, transformative action is illustrated in the biblical narrative of Ezra and Nehemiah. These transformative leaders led the Israelites in rebuilding and reforming Jerusalem after the exile. Their unwavering hope and certainty in Yahweh's faithfulness allowed this marginalized community to center itself and rebuild in the face of opposition. The word of God brought hope.

One of the principal themes of Ezra-Nehemiah is the relationship between God's work and human work. The book of Ezra begins with a decree from King Cyrus of Persia, allowing the Jews to return to Jerusalem to rebuild the temple. Cyrus made his proclamation "that the word of the LORD by the mouth of Jeremiah might be accomplished," and because "the LORD stirred up the spirit of King Cyrus" (Ezra 1:1). Cyrus was doing his work as king, seeking his personal and institutional ends, but God used him to bring about God's purposes. The fruit of this mission-focused spirituality is summed up in Nehemiah 4:6: "So we built the wall, and the entire wall was joined together up to half its height, for the people had a mind to work" (NKJV).

The passage shows God as motivator, as connector, and as protector. Seemingly effortless victories can occur when we practice mission-based spirituality. God brings us together and restores our hope, and people are motivated to get stuff done. This is the infectious type of ministry example that has driven me in my ministry and my leadership. It is so important to help people understand their role, get actively involved in the work, and know that God connects us all. As church leaders, we must know that God is in control, yet God works through his people, the church. God can even work through secular institutions and leaders, but it is the Spirit of God who generates the willingness, as he did with King Cyrus. The activated church leader needs to pray and be in tune with the Spirit. We must be ready when God speaks.

To fully live into its mission-focused spirituality, the activated church must adhere to these precepts:

1. *Proclaim the gospel of Jesus (Mark 16:15).* Christ is at the center of our work as Christians. Without the gospel, we are no different from any other nonprofit organization. Through our work, the love of God should flow out. The real difference made by an activated church comes through teaching people how to live out the gospel in their daily walk. It is not enough to preach "Love thy neighbor." How is the church demonstrating that in its programming and with its partnerships? The church must practice its proclamation.

2. *Regularly worship together (John 4:23-24).* We must show honor and praise to the God we serve. Worship binds us together as a community of believers, lifts us, and prepares us to receive from the Spirit of God. In an activated church, worship makes space for the marginalized and the "other." Worship is not treated as a members-only event, regardless of whether you are inviting people into the church or taking worship out into the community. One example of this can been seen in the ministry of Church Under the Bridge, a church for the homeless community in San Antonio. Their stated purpose is to reach out with the love of Jesus, giving hope through preaching, singing, and teaching the Word of God and offering training, free meals, and clothing to satisfy both the spiritual and physical needs of the congregation. Any congregation in San Antonio can sign up to participate in this ministry. The partnership allows for both the tangible proclamation of the gospel and worship with the "others" in the community.

3. *Intentionally point members toward discipleship (Matthew 28:19-20).* Discipleship models and guides others toward living righteously as followers of Jesus Christ. As we become disciples, we are called to disciple others. A crucial characteristic of being a disciple is developing an intimate relationship with God, not just learning about God. Discipleship equips the Christian with God's Word, prayer, doctrine, worship, encouragement, and service. In the next chapter, I go into more detail about discipleship and the activated church. An activated church masters the "walking alongside" part of discipleship. I love the fact that some twenty years later, kids whom I discipled still remember our journey. They often remember much more than I do.

4. *Set itself as a spiritual body and not just another community entity (Ephesians 6:12).* The apostle Paul reminds us that our battle is indeed spiritual, not physical. The challenges we face and the sources of opposition that seek to stop our work, ultimately, are not people or objects. The true opponent is sin in its many forms, especially as it seeks to divide people and destroy their hope. The activated church seeks balance between spirituality and social activism. Many churches fit the cliché of being so spiritual-minded that they are no earthly good. But others become so justice- or social-action minded that they are no good spiritually.

People think that if you work in a congregation, you have lots of time for prayer, meditation, and Bible study. That simply is not true. Many church leaders take their spiritual relationship for granted, or they only open the Bible to preach. Intentional spiritual self-care and discipline must be a priority for activated church leaders. We always need to center ourselves and our work.

5. *Use communal prayer and other spiritual disciplines as a form of discernment (1 Thessalonians 5:17).* As people of faith, we should believe that prayer makes a difference. Scientists and

psychologists have studied the benefits of prayer with mixed results, but as a Duke University study has suggested, the outcomes of the effects of "prayer treatments" must be taken seriously even though we can't prove that prayer works. Sometimes faith means going beyond statistical results.[1] A prayer team is just as important as an administrative team. I have experienced a lot of churches, and I've found that many people are okay with the church praying together, or with the pastoral team praying for the congregation. But the activated church has time set aside when everyone prays for each other and in groups. I remember my first concert of prayer. Many people were stressed out, did not know how to pray in small groups, and were self-conscious. Thankfully, the leader guided us in a way that helped move the prayer time along. After that, I was hooked, and I have used the process in other settings. Communal prayer is a very effective tool for bringing the church together and focusing on a common spiritual path. Dwelling in the Word is a similar practice, but I have chosen to focus on concerts of prayer and have added a sample outline for one in the resources section at the back of this book.

6. *Practice grace both inside and outside of the church body (Ephesians 2:8-9).* If we are not careful, the church can become an isolated holy huddle. We can become so self-righteous that we come to believe that it is our job, rather than the work of Christ, to save and to redeem people. God's grace saved us, and God's grace will work in the lives of others. We need to do our work with humility and compassion. Review your statements and your congregational discipline policies with this in mind. We, as a church body, must be mindful of our privilege and of the perception that others have of us. Is our unique identity sending a message of grace to those inside and outside the church?

7. *Embrace reconciliation, and not just simple forgiveness, as a key component of discipleship (2 Corinthians 5:16-21).* I have

heard people say that they can forgive, but won't forget. I love how Scripture lets us know that God has reconciled the world, and does not count people's sins against them. Reconciliation comes from the Greek family of words *allassō*, meaning "change" or "exchange." Reconciliation involves a change in the relationship between God and humankind or between person and person. Reconciliation moves us beyond the polarized thinking that divides us in the United States. The activated church does not see itself as "blue" or "red," as conservative or liberal, or as defined by the politics of this day. Practicing reconciliation means the church is committed to being in right relationship with people inside the church and those in the community. This is not a call to tolerate sin or evil, but it means caring enough to seek God and confront unresolved issues with an open mind, desiring to improve the relationship.

I believe the activated church will be slow to draw lines in the sand. Instead of casting judgment based on specific issues and seeking to "eliminate" people from relationships, the activated church provides structures for dialogue and education. The activated church works to take a deeper dive into understanding the roots from which conflicting perspectives on issues spring. The church becomes a place of mutual spiritual accountability, not condemnation (Romans 8:1-4). There is a fine line between accountability and condemnation. As we walk together in the discipling relationship, accountability is about mutual support and growth. Condemnation comes from a place of superiority and control. In the relationship of accountability, we grow together. In the relationship of condemnation, we slowly chip away at the identity of others to re-create them in our image.

Listening to the Spirit should guide the actions of the church. I asked Pastor Enrique how his congregation engages their community. He said, "Even though we are a spiritual organization, we want to be the physical representation of Christ on earth. We get involved in the city cleanup day. We have joined with other religious leaders in the city on the clergy committee. We meet with Catholics, Christians, and different types of faith leaders who meet [together]. We can get information on what is going on in the city. We want to understand what the needs are." Enrique went on to say, "For instance, just this week there was a fire in an apartment complex in which the grandfather and father were killed, leaving behind a five-year-old kid. Members of the committee were able to go minister to that family."

I asked Pastor Enrique if there was ever a time when people said his church was too spiritual. "Well, there is always resistance," he replied. "You know we wrestle not against flesh and blood. Some say we pray too much or that we are too spiritual. But people want to go to the extreme in the other direction. 'Let's be a church that feeds the hungry. Let's give to the poor.' Of course, we are going to do those things, but every church needs a strong focus. If you love the Lord, you're automatically going to serve, and you're automatically going to be moved by compassion to help people. But we can go to the extreme when you talk about serving or trying to be engaged in the community. I see some churches that are so locked into social programs, they are no longer a church. They are just another service organization."

I understood what Pastor Enrique was saying. Two things jump out to me. First, he pointed out that each church has an area of focus. His statement affirms my belief that the activated church understands its identity and its role within the community. Second, while service and reaching out to the poor are essential functions of the church, the church isn't just another community social service institution. It is our spiritual nature that sets us apart. Scripture and our love of Christ drive us to have compassion, but the church not only seeks to change peoples' physical condition; it also exists as a place of spiritual transformation and reconciliation.

Pastor Enrique shared additional observations. "I see some pastors on Instagram and Facebook, and sometimes I wonder when they have time for prayer and spiritual disciplines. I'm sweating twelve hours, studying, trying to get my Sunday sermon together, and it looks like they are on social media all the time. I have a desperation for God. I understand using new technology, but the old technology of prayer is fine. Just get on your knees and pray. An old pastor once told me, 'Your iPhone can't fast and pray for you.'" I love that last piece of wisdom, and it made me laugh out loud.

In the chapter on SEO (that is, seeker-engaging organization), I talked a lot about technology and how we need to embrace it as an essential tool in our ministry. I emphasized engaging young people in the communities that they are part of, the online community of cell phones and social media. I stick by that even after hearing Pastor Enrique's critique. Using technology doesn't mean we shouldn't also spend time on our knees in prayer. We still need to spend time talking to God. That's why this chapter is included. I have incorporated technology into my spiritual preparation. I have apps that play the Scriptures as I meditate on the Word of God. I use my iPad to play hymns to keep me focused and awake when I pray. Various other apps help me look at different translations of the Bible as well as the Greek and Hebrew of certain passages. When I am finished, I may text or post a Scripture verse that I found helpful that day, sharing the verse with friends and family. Technology itself is not inherently good or bad. We should find the tools that are most helpful for our consistency.

While most of my conversation with Pastor Enrique focused on prayer, he also pointed out the importance of Bible study in his preparation and the work of his ministry. Although it may not seem obvious, the development of our minds plays an important role in our spiritual development. In some cultures, pastors have tried to downplay education and its relationship to spiritual growth. I grew up hearing several Black pastors calling seminary "the cemetery," because they believed it killed your faith. While I understand the roots of that sentiment, I also now understand why it is nonsense. For spiritual transformation to occur, the activated church must include education as part of its mission-focused spirituality. J. P. Moreland writes, "If I want to change my beliefs about something, I embark on a course of study in which I choose to think regularly about certain things, read certain pieces of evidence and argument, and try to find problems with evidence raised against the belief in question."[2] Spirituality is about awareness, not ignorance. We have too many narrow-minded Christians who are not fed by the Holy Spirit, and who are being manipulated and kept in the dark by deceitful shepherds. As Hosea prophesies, "My people are destroyed for lack of knowledge; because you have rejected knowledge, I reject you from being a priest to me. And since you have forgotten the law of your God, I also will forget your children" (Hosea 4:6).

Intellectual growth and effective spiritual growth should go hand in hand in the activated church. The activated church leader who wants to grow spiritually will also seek wisdom and knowledge. As part of our mission-focused spirituality, we need to study for spiritual growth, intellectual growth, and the improvement of our skills. The knowledge we gain is like fertilizing the spiritual fields of our mind so that when the Spirit speaks or plants ideas, they go into good, receptive ground. We can act on the information because we have prepared ourselves for it. Missionary J. Oswald Sanders wrote, "Sometimes the ignorance of our minds hinders our prayers. But the Spirit knows the mind of God and shares that knowledge with us as we wait and listen."[3] If our minds are not ready, we handicap the Spirit. We handicap ourselves.

QUESTIONS FOR REFLECTION

1. What are the unmet needs in your community? (Often politicians, medical professionals, educators, or other local leaders will be able to highlight these.)

2. How well are social service organizations in your community meeting the demands?

3. Are your mission or outreach resources being directed to the most urgent need gaps in your community?

4. Do your members have any unique gifts or skills that can meet the most urgent needs in your community?

5. What percentage of your church budget is directed toward external mission versus general operations? Are you sending at least 10 percent of your budget outside your walls?

FIVE

Characteristic Three:

Intentional Discipleship and Faith Formation Strategy

Therefore, go and make disciples of all the nations, baptizing them in the name of the Father and the Son and the Holy Spirit. Teach these new disciples to obey all the commands I have given you. And be sure of this: I am with you always, even to the end of the age.
—MATTHEW 28:19-20 (NLT)

DISCIPLESHIP IS SYNONYMOUS with discipline and self-control, but disciples do not achieve control through reading or through memorizing a litany of rules. As we think about discipleship, we must look at the roots of this term as used by the early church. The term *disciple* is a translation of the

Greek word *mathētēs*, learner. A learner is one who engages in learning through instruction from another person, a teacher. Discipleship is not only about the pupil or apprentice, but about the relationship between the learner and the teacher. True discipleship is a formative and close relationship. The disciple and the teacher are invariably closely associated with one another. The teacher should be a mature person who has a pedagogical reputation or a set of views; in other words, a discipline (purpose) for the disciple. Activated churches are seeking change, but not from the Oval Office or some impersonal bureaucracy. Lasting change comes from helping people see that, despite our flaws, we are all connected through the Spirit. We equip people for leadership in the community via discipleship and partnerships with healthy role models. When explosive situations manifest themselves, the church can be at the center of managing the ecology of change in a way that builds upon the strength of the community rather than destroying the community through reactionary violence and mistrust.

There are three benefits to discipleship that ultimately enhance the ability of the activated church to engage the community and facilitate transformation:

DISCIPLESHIP PROVIDES ACCOUNTABILITY

First Corinthians 12:27 reminds us that we are part of the body of Christ; we are also essential individual parts of that body. Through discipleship, members find not only their fit, but how they connect to their church and the larger universal church of Christ. As the famous poet John Donne says, we are not islands unto ourselves, we are part of something bigger. Discipleship and other forms of faith formation facilitate that connectivity. We find out we are not alone in our walk. Through discipleship, we find a sense of accountability and reciprocity in our relationship with other believers. We cannot be tempted as believers to think our faith can fully mature in isolation. No, this Christian faith is about the breathed Spirit of God flowing through each of us and connecting us to God.

Discipleship also helps us be open to wise counsel from a friend, pastor, or spouse, people who God may use for our protection. Hopefully, discipleship also protects us from those who want to use misinformation, deception, and spirituality to harm.

DISCIPLESHIP BUILDS COMMUNITY

Coming together is at the heart of this Christian walk. As my interview later in this chapter points out, when we practice true discipleship, it is automatically connected to the community, and that community is often tiered. There are different levels of community and relationships, the degree of accountability changing at each of the levels. The body of Christ is simply not meant to exist only as a gathering on Sundays. We shouldn't be in the practice of disengaging and then moving along with our lives for the rest of the week. How powerful would it be if the church of the twenty-first century lived in a community like the early church did? Scripture paints a picture of believers doing life together (Acts 2:44-47).

Seeking counsel and discipleship is one way to invite others into your life. The church of today might be too hands-off, too disconnected from its members. People drop in and drive out. There is no real community other than the "passing of the peace" or the isolating greetings of first-time visitors. These interactions are short, scripted, and often embarrassing to introverted people. In the South, where I grew up, fellowship was long and drawn out and most often occurred over food. No one was in a rush to leave. Those practices remind us that church was once more a central part of our lives than it is today. Those days of slow fellowship on Sunday afternoons may be a bygone era for most churches, but that does not mean the church of today can't be creative in the ways it uses technology or gathers at alternate locations to build a sense of intimate community.

DISCIPLESHIP EQUIPS US

The apostle Paul reminds us in Titus 2 that it is the responsibility of the older generation to teach the next generation what is right and to equip the youth to walk in step with the truth of the gospel. Discipleship is not about using empty words, but is about walking alongside a person or a group of people and mentoring them in preparation for what comes next.

For this chapter, I spoke with Pastor Charles, a young youth pastor with experience in several different congregations who has good relationships with youth ministry practitioners and youth from across the country. I was interested in hearing his philosophy of discipleship, since at heart I am still a youth pastor, and I recognize effective youth leaders when I see them. They excel at the call of mentoring and successfully guiding young people toward transformation.

Pastor Charles got his start watching his father and uncle pastor churches. While Pastor Charles has no formal seminary training, he was mentored and discipled by members of his family. Pastor Charles shared, "My greatest passion in ministry is walking with people and having meaningful conversations. These conversations occur while taking people through ordered journeys with me, not just telling them about ministry, but allowing them to experience ministry." Pastor Charles reflected that the discipleship example of his father stirred his passion for ministry and a desire to share that passion with others. "My dad always did some type of outreach in the community when I was growing up. We would go out into the city. I remember the feeling of being involved in the implementation of ministry was a whole lot more meaningful than just going to church, sitting and hearing about what God could do. Seeing the church making a difference and being a part of that work was so much more powerful."

Discipleship for Pastor Charles was packing up the van on snowy Saturday mornings, grabbing a cup of hot chocolate, and going to meet people in their place of need. This is the image of the church ingrained in the mind of this young pastor. He then shared with me the moment he realized this act of discipleship was the way that Jesus formed his band of disciples. "When I thought of the ministry I wanted to do, I started connecting the stories I read of Jesus. I began to see the parallels between what my father had done to exactly what Jesus was doing. Jesus was gathering up a bunch of young guys and saying, 'Hey, let's go out there and make a difference in people's lives. Let's go where we are needed and be the solution.' As they walked and served, there would be moments along the way where Jesus would stop and talk up to his disciples, teach them, and show them why they were doing what they were doing."

I like to call this dirty discipleship—going out, using your hands. Pastor Charles points out that the Sadducees were the elite, discipled in ivory towers far away from the needs of the community. For those who followed Jesus, discipleship and faith formation happened amid active ministry. While Scripture points out times when Jesus was in the synagogue, the miracles of Jesus occurred on the road, in community. Jesus did ministry/service, then afterward reflected on the *why* with his disciples. The teaching and learning were part of the intentional process of engaging with communities in need. Why do I say that this kind of discipleship is dirty? When you are walking with people and serving, you will have moments of frustration and challenges. But if you want to move the mountains of oppression, sickness, financial stress, and poverty, you must be there in the muck and the mire. You must be face-to-face with the community and the dirtiness of having people close, walking with you.

Pastor Charles described the next part of this kind of discipleship: "But then you get to experience the beauty of seeing them transformed and empowered to do ministry for others." He calls this a Red Bull moment; the spiritual term probably would be closer to *kairos*, that passing instant when an opening appears which must be driven through with force if we want to achieve success. It is the formative moment when the walking produces its wings (as in the Red Bull commercials), and the disciple can take off. I imagine young people being released from the tension of not knowing who they are or their purpose and breaking away from the unhealthy, limiting tethers of this world. Pastor Charles said, "I've seen kids who are really quiet, who didn't know what their voice sounded like, find their voice to discipleship, and so those are some of the kids that have become a leader even in youth ministry." This active, dirty discipleship allows God to use them, and then they start to crave being used by God. They want to share that awesome experience with others. Red Bull gives you wings, but serving activates a desire in disciples to actively carry out the great commission.

The activated church must find creative ways to get people involved in ministry. Sitting in on a Sunday or Wednesday church service is not creating disciples. Am I suggesting that you not have Sunday or Wednesday services? No, of course not, but those worship experiences will not lead to the fulfillment of the great commission. Church leaders must create experiences where people feel ownership in the work of the church. Many religious services today are clean, pristine, overly choreographed events. Many attendees are spectators. Worship is produced like the Dove Awards, and we project words on the HD screen, hoping folks can follow along. We are not even taking the time to connect on a deeper level with people who show up to worship, much less providing opportunities to practice the intimacy necessary to create disciples.

I asked Pastor Charles to define discipleship. "In its simplicity," he said, "discipleship is helping people understand what it means to follow Christ, and then showing them how to help others follow Christ. If you are successful, then you create a cycle of disciples making disciples. You want to create a system [where] people are following the example of Jesus and are walking alongside others who need that same example."

Pastor Charles acknowledged the importance of individuals and intentional relationships in the process. We need to act as ambassadors or liaisons between Christ and people in need. "So we are ambassadors for Christ, since God is making his appeal through us; we entreat you on behalf of Christ, be reconciled to God" (2 Corinthians 5:20). I think Pastor Charles is correct in saying, "Often they start out thinking that they're following me around, but what they end up discovering is that we're following Christ together, and then that becomes what they take to the next generation, or the next friend." Pastor Charles isn't saying that we are to be worshiped and take the place of God or that we should go on some type of ego trip, turning people into indentured servants. I believe he is capturing the true essence of discipleship and leadership. We need to reflect Christ's love, and we are most effective in reaching people with whom we have an affinity, which is why churches need to pay attention to diversity and inclusion and to be aware of the culture of their communities. One ongoing question is, Can you be effective in the community in which you are serving? Are you able to connect with and walk alongside the people who are in need?

Pastor Charles's strategy of gaining followers while being a follower isn't groundbreaking. It is modeled after the life and interactions of Christ. It is simplicity, and its biblical founda-

Figure 5.1. **Circles of relation**

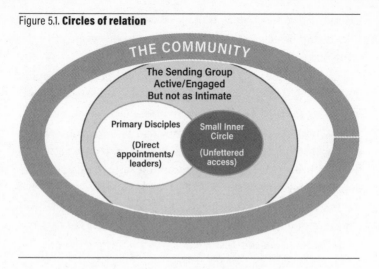

tions are what make it impactful. As Jesus walked with the disciples, there were various levels of intimacy and transparency that Jesus had with them.

Jesus had his three closest disciples and inner circle family; he had the twelve disciples, and the seventy, and then there was the crowd. With each group, there was a decreasing level of intimacy and personal sharing as the circle got larger. But they all walked with Jesus and were connected. Each group had a function in the work of Jesus; the inner circle supported the heart of the work (Jesus), and the twelve executed the vision and helped manage those in the sending group, the seventy. The community, or the crowd, was the place of engagement. In the outer circle, broad needs were met, and the foundations for deeper discipleship began. There must be a core leadership team that helps cement and set the vision, but that team must be backed by other trained leaders who are disciplined and feel ownership for the work of the congregation.

Everyone needs discipleship. The groups that walked with Jesus included men and women. As the apostle Mark points out,

"There were also women looking on from a distance; among them were Mary Magdalene, and Mary the mother of James the younger and Joses, and Salome. These used to follow him and provided for him when he was in Galilee; and there were many other women who had come up with him to Jerusalem" (Mark 15:40-41). Too often, the church sees discipleship as a masculine exercise of faith, but the Scriptures highlight many great miracles and teaching occurring as Jesus interacted with women. The church needs to incorporate more women in its mentoring and discipleship programs. Keep in mind that discipleship and formative training need to be age appropriate. They need to happen intentionally for all those who are members of a congregation or other ministry group.

THE LEGACY POTENTIAL OF DIRTY DISCIPLESHIP

While I was sheltering in my home like the rest of America during the global pandemic, I happened to tune into a Facebook Live event hosted by a former student of mine. The student was DJing in his backyard. So I decided to watch as I was finishing up this book. I gave him a few likes and requested a few songs. The student obliged my "old school" request and started to give me a few shoutouts during his presentation. I probably watched and listened for an hour or so, requesting a song here or there. At one point, his young son stepped into view. A few minutes later, a cream-colored Fender guitar also entered the view. To my surprise, my former student went on to say that I had given him this guitar, and now he had passed the guitar down to his son. That gift had been given some twenty years ago. I do not remember that transaction, but I do remember sitting with this young man and his sisters when he was a teenager and their father died. He reminded me of the one-on-one talks I had with him during his time of grief. Now some of the physical and spiritual gifts I shared with him were being passed on to his son.

These are the stories that pop up at random when I come across my ministry kids, who now range in age from their thirties to forties. They talk about the impact the ministry had on their lives and how they are using those lessons now. The stories they share somehow always involve the conversations and the kindness we shared. I don't think anyone has ever said, "Remember when you preached about . . ." Maybe I need more memorable sermons—or maybe the heart of discipleship is loving and caring for each other, with Christ at the center of the relationship. Similarly, when I talked to Pastor Charles about discipleship, my heart was warmed as he described discipleship as drinking hot chocolate on a winter's day with his dad. That is what changes lives and cements the gospel in our hearts.

I remember fondly how my spiritual mentors touched my life, and I am humbled by the opportunity to have a similar impact on others. In addition to biblical lessons, the times I remember are the trips, the deep conversations, and the talks over lunch or coffee. That one-on-one discipleship has lifted me over the years. The one-on-one time let me know that my mentors practiced what they preached. They believed the stuff they were sharing. One-on-one discipleship and the mutual accountability it involves has been the one spiritual discipline that continually reminds me of who I am and the responsibility I have as a member of the clergy and as a person of faith. Age notwithstanding, images of Matthew 18:6, which warns against putting a stumbling block before one of God's little ones, come to my mind as I think about what a precious gift it is to be called to disciple someone. It is unconscionable to abuse power and trust granted to you in that role. Sadly, this is part of the danger of these deep ministry relationships.

How do we prevent abuse in discipleship relationships? I don't believe we should eliminate one-on-one discipleship, nor do I think the disciple relationship should be exclusive. I have a bit of a bias. I have had great, great spiritual mentors. Because of my military background and probably because my mom was so outspoken, I have never been afraid to question authority. To a certain extent, I have had the skill to protect myself from bad leaders. Everyone's background and warning "radar" works differently. The mentor relationship must be built on trust and with some wisdom. When churches engage in discipleship, I suggest the following steps to prevent the relationship from sliding into manipulation or even abuse (including abuse of power or sexual abuse):

- Run background checks on leaders, especially those working with youth.

- Have a combination of group and individual components to the discipleship program.

- Have an official outline of the discipleship relationship and program. It is important not to allow the emotional nature of the relationship to move to unhealthy codependency or romance.

- Have an evaluation process or check-in to monitor relationships.

- Place women in leadership roles.

- Train your discipleship leadership team on healthy boundaries, racism, and sexual abuse as appropriate.

Can you have mixed-gender groups? That is a culturally loaded question, so I can't answer that for every reader. I do reject the old philosophy that a Christian man can never be alone with a Christian woman without something naughty happening. Also, there are many people involved in same-gender partnerships or dating relationships, so gender segregation is no magic cure to prevent abusive relationships. (Abuse can occur within any relationship between two or more people.) The cure to healthy discipleship relationships is providing good training, selecting good people, and active monitoring. Remember, the activated church has an *intentional* (planned, well-thought-out) discipleship and faith formation strategy.

Let's go out on a limb and imagine that Matthew 28:19-28 is a "great commission" for all churches. Imagine churches have adopted this as their primary mission. Where then should our time and energy be devoted? Matthew 28 refers to discipleship, which should not be confused with congregational member-ship. Matthew 28 calls the disciples to observe and practice the stuff that Jesus did. I wonder how much time Jesus spent in committee meetings. Did Jesus and his disciples spend the bulk of their time coming up with an excellent Sunday service, or did they spend more time defending the persecuted? Jesus was engaged in the community. He was on the streets; he walked among the people, sharing with them messages that related di-rectly to their context. Jesus spoke to the situations people were in, whether they were fishermen, homemakers, soldiers, cooks, or farmers.

Too much of our time is spent planting and sustaining sep-arate congregations. If our true goal as an activated church is to be a place of transformation and of building nurturing rela-tionships, we should not put so many of our resources and so much of our energy into managing real estate. Are we build-ing churches to be effective ministers of the gospel, or are we building ego edifices with overhead that we cannot afford? Hear me: A congregation does need a physical place to meet, but that place does not have to be a five-hundred-seat cathedral. I think about what happened during the global pandemic of 2020. Many congregations were not prepared to care for their members during the period of social distancing; aside from the pressure of paying bills, many pastors had questions about how

Figure 5.2. **Support structure of a common use facility**

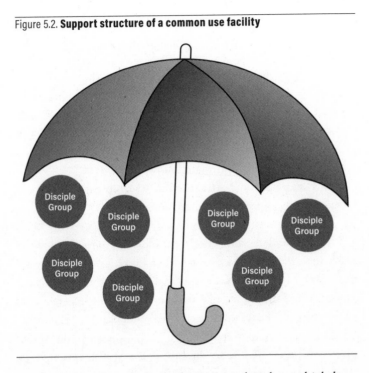

to engage members. I think about megachurches, which have a lot of invisible members who are not well known. These are members who float in and float out and have no real connection to people at the church.

Megachurches with large, expensive facilities may have a purpose, but smaller congregations and house churches do have some benefits.

- They are nimbler and can shift to meet community needs more easily.

- They are not restricted by money or funding.

- Great emphasis is placed on relationships.

- Often, they are simple in their approach.

- There is greater accountability between individual members.
- It is easier to practice intentional discipleship.

Ultimately, we should develop the type of church that works effectively in our community in laying the foundations for Christian discipleship and transformation. In some cases, it may be denominational partnerships, house churches, cell groups, or some networked hybrid of independent ministries who partner together and share resources.

How we gather and structure our worship experiences will have a direct impact on our mission-focused spirituality. We pray and worship to communicate and connect with God. J. Oswald Sanders said, "Both natural and spiritual qualities reach their greatest effectiveness when employed in the service of God and for his glory. Yet spiritual leadership transcends the power or personality and all other natural gifts. The personality of the spiritual leader influences others because it is penetrated, saturated, and empowered by the Holy Spirit. As the leader gives control of his life to the Spirit, the Spirit's power flows through [the leader] to others."[1]

If churches had the mindset that discipleship was a primary focus, we would organize churches a lot differently. We could share facilities and operational support while intentionally focusing our strengths instead of providing a buffet of programs with stressed and poorly trained volunteers. One would hope that denominationalism or cell church models would solve the problem of support, but what often happens is that the denominational bureaucracy, the middle adjudicatory, and the local congregation become competitors for a limited amount of resources. We need a new, networked hybrid model that deemphasizes large production as the norm and focuses on ministering to smaller groups.

QUESTIONS FOR REFLECTION

1. Can you be effective in your local community?

2. Are you able to connect with and walk alongside the people who are in need?

3. What types of intentional affinity groups do you have to promote spiritual intimacy?

4. How easy is it for people to get involved in church service programs?

5. Do you have age-appropriate discipleship opportunities?

6. Do you have resources to equip parents to disciple their children?

SIX

Characteristic Four:
Intentional Diversity and Inclusion

For it was you who formed my inward parts;
you knit me together in my mother's womb.
I praise you, for I am fearfully and wonderfully made.
Wonderful are your works;
that I know very well.
—PSALM 139:13-14

ACTIVATED CHURCHES DEVELOP and relate to a diverse Christian community, thereby facilitating an intercultural community. The church is often an amalgamation of people with different expectations and experiences. Getting along under a single umbrella is not always easy, but successful churches figure it out. There are many ways to embrace diversity and inclusion. Intentional diversity and inclusion should start with the question, "Do our programs, practices, and population reflect God's love at work in this community?" Inclusive diversity is hard to get right, but the church needs to lean in to the journey. The handful of congregations I have seen master diversity and inclusion have set that as a goal early in the formation of the ministry. Those congregations are also in population settings that foster diversity. You have to be in touch with the opportunities and needs of your community (we'll get to that a little bit later).

Please be mindful that when thinking about diversity and inclusion, your context matters. Diversity and inclusion in the context of ministry are not about "How do *we* get more of *them* into our building?" Knowing your identity is closely related to how we execute our diversity and inclusion goals. We always need to be open to the move of God and growth that connects us to the communities we serve and those on the margins who might need us.

The activated church gains a shared sense of grace, practices courteous goodwill to others, and acknowledges God's favor rather than human-based superiority as it works on developing intercultural competencies. Church leaders need to develop skills that can help dismantle systemic, cross-cultural, and intra-cultural racism. The activated church can be a refuge or oasis from systemic forms of oppression experienced in other settings, a community where believers can get a sense of who they are and where God is calling them. The church must reflect God in a way that affirms others. We all bring different pieces of our identity with us as we fellowship and worship.

There is a common analogy that I strongly dislike because I think it misses the mark. I'll share it with you in hopes of killing it off and replacing it with a better analogy. Here's what popular wisdom says:

Diversity is being invited to the party.

Inclusion is being asked to dance.

I hate this analogy for several reasons. First, it never gives the "other" any ownership in what is happening. It's not their party, and they can't dance unless the host asks them. Second, the example is so patriarchal. Is the party guest some dainty belle from the antebellum South waiting for Rhett Butler to rescue her from plantation life? Third, how do I know your dance style or the style of music is something that inspires me to dance? You could be asking me to do the Cotton-Eyed Joe, a Texas favorite, but maybe I am more of a ballroom kind of person. I prefer this modified version of the analogy:

Diversity is attending a party with lots of different people.

Inclusion is being a member of the planning team, helping select the DJ, the menu, and sharing your playlist.

Intercultural competency is the communication and management system you use to make it all happen.

DIVERSITY AND THE IMAGE OF GOD

Through transformation, people can see who they are in God's eyes, not only in the eyes of the world. To get there, the church must reflect the *imago Dei*, the image of God. Things will change as a church moves from homogeneity to becoming a more diverse and inclusive body of worship. You must be intentional about these changes and how you will meet the evolving needs of your congregation. That is one of the reasons why I recommend that congregations who want to practice intentional diversity and inclusion begin with identifying their starting point. What are the opportunities and stretch points of your congregation? I find most churches get stuck right here. Their model of diversity is the assimilation model: Join us, and we will change you. They want people who appear outwardly different but fit a narrow mold. Instead of the *imago Dei*, they want the corporate culture of the congregation to be preeminent because that is what is comfortable for them. I am not trying to contradict what I said about a church having a unique identity or culture, but I am saying that we cannot "whitewash" or erase the unique gifts of the individuals who make up our congregations. We don't want Stepford members (see Ira Levin's 1972 novel turned feature film). Unity is found in our Christian mission and service. Church unity is not achieved by our members becoming conforming, submissive robots.

There can be unity of vision and mission amid other aspects of diversity. We can be at the same party and dance differently. If we do this right, together, we can create some new moves. We are an increasingly identity-driven society. Millennials and Gen Zers carry their awareness of identity much differently than past generations. You should not just randomly start throwing "diversity" parties and hope they are a spiritual field of dreams—"If we build it, they will come." I say, who are *they*, where are *they* coming from, and why would *they* want to come to your party? Preparation is essential.

GET THE RIGHT LEADERSHIP

One critical aspect of diversity is ensuring that the leadership of an activated church reflects the people in the pews and the community. The leadership also needs to be open to the diversity that you are seeking. I have seen churches split over all types of diversity issues. The activated church must be committed to the cultural shifts and resistance that working at diversity can bring—that is why it is easier to plan for diversity in the formation stage of a congregation. There are fewer institutional barriers to dismantle. The right leadership team will also have a diverse set of skills and the cultural understanding to plan for what will happen at your party. If the leadership isn't inclusive, you are not practicing diversity and inclusion; you are planning a good old antebellum South cotillion and asking folks to dance to your music.

SET THE RIGHT DIVERSITY GOAL

What is the goal that is achievable for your context? In the resources section, I have put together a list of some identity targets that you can wrestle with for your congregation. Do you want to be more inclusive based on race, gender, physical identity, or another trait or traits? Where is God calling you, and where are your skills aligned? For me, racial, gender, and generational diversity are always part of my leadership strategy. I don't have the skills at this point to work effectively with non-English speakers, at least not at the level of competency I desire. Nor am I in touch with many people with disabilities. There are times when I work outside the populations with whom I have higher levels of competency, but I call in experts to assist me in understanding these groups. Based on my skills, my area of calling, and the requirements of a role, I determine which areas are not my primary areas of diversity work. The key takeaways here are that you can't work at everything at the same level of proficiency. But you can be skilled enough to remove barriers and be open to help when you need it. If I were speaking to my corporate clients who are asking how to reach their diversity goals, I would tell them to think about three areas: talent acquisition, talent retention, and talent development. Since churches are not corporations, let me adjust those key areas for the ministry context.

Talent acquisition, or expanding your pool. Two opportunities for churches that will spur growth and diversity are strategic partnerships and alternative meeting locations. If you want to be diverse, it is best to have the biggest pool of participants possible. Certain traditions, affiliations, and locations will limit the size of your pool. That is reality. Intentional diversity and inclusion strategies expand a small pond of potential talent into an ocean of potential talent or, in the case of the church, members. Fishing in the ocean gives you many more options than fishing in a small pond. Intentional diversity and inclusion practices help you find people in regions and locations that you may normally overlook.

- Set up ministry locations or services in a non-churchy location such as a park, a bar, a school, or online.

- Join with other ministries that are struggling or with whom you can share resources, people, and knowledge.

- Consider a satellite location or additional campus to connect with people from different demographics.

If your pool is small, you may have to look beyond the usual spaces and places and search the uncharted waters. Who knows what relationships you will build? During the protests and civil unrest related to the 2020 killing of George Floyd, many church leaders and politicians said that America must turn to God to heal racism. The lieutenant governor of Texas said that we need a culture change to address racism and that we cannot change the culture of the country until we change humanity's character. In the Christian community, too many of us are quick to offer thoughts and prayers. Too many Christians who offer platitudes about harmony are members of racially segregated congregations. Empty words from leaders are not enough. It takes hard, hands-on work to change—dare I say to transform—the culture. We need a diverse community of Christian disciples who are accountable to each other and working together. We need discipleship relationships that cross cultures. I have hope that we can help end racism when our faith communities become more diverse and empowering.

Talent retention, or member retention. Strong diversity initiatives combined with strong inclusion practices will help foster an environment where groups in the minority will want to stay with your congregation, and they will tell their friends that this is a great place to worship. Happy members are more productive and stay with the congregation longer. Everyone benefits. I recommend getting people involved in leadership. Think back to the party analogy. It is not enough to be a good host. Let people make your congregation home; let it become their congregation. Practice cultural competence.

Talent development, or discipleship. If you want great diversity, sometimes you must develop it. Ministry programs can attract diverse people to congregations. There are even leadership programs in many denominations that allow you to mentor future leaders. Take advantage of these programs. Use these opportunities to build long-term discipleship relationships that may lead to better diversity and inclusion in the local congregation. In the corporate world, there are often internships and training programs for underrepresented groups. There is no reason that the church should not consider similar strategies. "Discipleship" is just what we have named our spiritual mentorship programs and educational partnerships.

GET THE RIGHT KNOWLEDGE

Knowledge is important once you start throwing your diversity party. Get the information you need to achieve your goals so that you can dismantle the cultural barriers that exclude, offend, and marginalize people. Intercultural competency is the system, the toolbox of knowledge and processes, that allows diversity and inclusion to work. The authors of a toolkit on building culturally competent organizations outline the following levels of cultural competency[1]:

1. *Cultural knowledge* means that you know about some cultural characteristics, history, values, beliefs, and behaviors of another ethnic or cultural group.

2. *Cultural awareness* is the next stage of understanding other groups—being open to the idea of changing cultural attitudes.

3. *Cultural sensitivity* is knowing that differences exist between cultures, but not assigning values to the differences (better or worse, right or wrong). Clashes on this point can easily occur, especially if a custom or belief in question goes against the idea of multiculturalism. Internal conflict (intrapersonal, interpersonal, and organizational) is likely to occur at times over this issue. Conflict won't always be easy to manage, but it can be made easier if everyone is mindful of the organizational goals.

4. *Cultural competence* brings together the previous stages— and adds operational effectiveness. A culturally competent organization can bring into its system many different behaviors, attitudes, and policies, and [can] work effectively in cross-cultural settings to produce better outcomes.[2]

INTERCULTURAL COMMUNICATION AND CONGREGATIONS

One of the biggest barriers we face as institutions is communicating across our differences. Intercultural communication is very important if we are seeking to reach a diverse audience, and we want to practice effective inclusion. If we don't recognize communication barriers and the different cultural communication styles, we can foster conflict within our communities. People experience this conflict as an emotional struggle between different groups. The feelings increase during times of crisis because there is a shortage. The shortage can be real or perceived; either way, it creates tension that distracts leaders from doing important work. It can manifest in a shortage of access to information, vital resources, present or future opportunity, or resources for safety and well-being.

Intercultural competency is an important practice for the activated church. Intercultural competence is the systemic ability to function effectively across cultures, to think and act appropriately, and to communicate and work with people from different cultural backgrounds. It is the "how" as we think about diversity and inclusion. As congregations work with more diverse populations, here are few things to consider in improving communication between groups.

1. Bring in trusted leaders/influencers to help with communication and change management.

2. Translate/interpret information as appropriate to address language and accessibility issues.

3. Clear, concise information is best; don't wing it when you are sharing information about new programs or important decisions.

4. Check in with groups who in the past have complained or who have expressed concerns regarding communication.

5. Understand that different cultures have different leadership expectations. Show your face. Let people see you and show empathy and concern.

6. During times of crisis or conflict, overcommunicate. People want to know what is going on. If you don't provide enough information, people will make up information.

7. Be honest. "We don't have that answer yet" is better than telling a lie.

During times of crisis and conflict, the amount of "background" noise increases. People who are stressed are not as receptive as calm people. Keep this in mind as you share information.

Figure 6.1. **Intercultural competency common use facility**

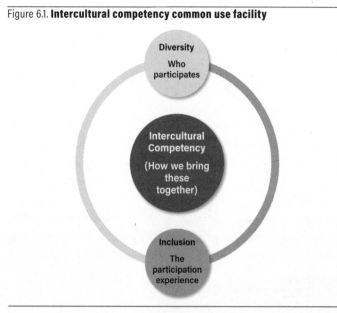

A second part, maybe the most important part of strategic diversity and inclusion, is understanding inclusion as part of the work of biblical reconciliation. Not only must we believe that we are all created in the image of God and that God is in us, but we must also acknowledge that as a collective of members, we are all unified in Christ.

RECONCILIATION AND INCLUSION

A significant part of transformation is understanding the what and why of who we are. Ultimately, we are the sum of our choices, our experiences, and our environment. The great part about accepting Christ is that transformation is a spiritual transaction that sets us right with God. We are reconciled. Despite our unique identity factors and experiences, we are set right with God and become part of this body. We are included. "From now on, therefore, we regard no one from a human point of view; even though we once knew Christ from a human point of view, we know him no longer in that way. So if anyone is in Christ, there is a new creation: everything old has passed away; see, everything has become new! All this is from God, who reconciled us to himself through Christ, and has given us the ministry of reconciliation" (2 Corinthians 5:16-18).

The activated church understands that not only do we individually invite Christ into our hearts, but the collective with which we become one is the body of Christ. The activated church has room for all because it has the theological understanding to say, "Our identity is that of being joined to Christ." This goes beyond our individual biases, customs, and traditions. The activated church, therefore, can be more inclusive of the traditions and diverse understanding of others. Diversity is no

Figure 6.2. **Ministry of reconciliation**

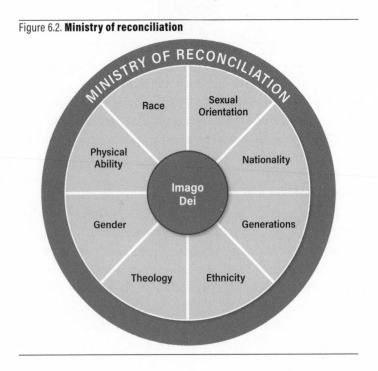

longer a limitation or a problem to be solved, but an opportunity to celebrate the "bigness" of God. Klyne Snodgrass, a New Testament scholar, says, "If Christ is only in you, then how big is Christ? Not very big, and you can tuck him away when you don't need him. But, if you and all other human beings are in Christ as well as all of Creation, then how big is Christ?"[3]

Although your church maybe welcoming and inviting to many different folks, the church is rooted in cultural traditions. I get that, and you should too before proclaiming victory too soon. Cultural bias does not evaporate overnight. We must continually work at reconciliation.

Here are six tips for building an inclusive culture, fostering a sense of belonging in your congregation.

1. *Get the right people in the room.* The composition of the planning group or leadership team makes a difference in the successful execution of any attempt to create a culture of inclusion. Like biological cultures in yogurt or sourdough bread, the right "starter" makes a difference. The first step in promoting diversity and inclusion that supports a sense of belonging for members is starting with a diverse and inclusive planning or leadership team. The leadership group must represent the constituency. You can't be an inclusive body without the willingness to share power and control. Empowering marginalized and underrepresented people will change who you are. It will shift your culture. If you are not willing to share power, don't lie to yourself, claiming that you are interested in diversity and inclusion. Just rip this chapter out of the book and be a semi-engaged church rather than an activated church. Here are some questions to ask:

- Who is constructing the leadership team? What does it look like demographically compared to the church mission and demographics?

- Does the leadership team represent the groups who will be engaged in worship or other programs?

- Who is not invited to help with planning? Why is that?

- What assumptions about leadership and worship does the dominant culture have?

- What orientation is provided for (new) members of the leadership team? Is someone assigned as a mentor for new members or attendees to help them get familiarized?

2. *Get specific.* Communicate what success looks like for your ministry. I define culture as "the way we do things around here." Clearly define for your group what it means to have a culture of inclusion and belonging. Only you can define what type of diversity is right for you. That is why I included the resource "Identity Factors That May Affect Your Diversity and Inclusion Efforts" in the back of the book. Often we focus on race and ethnicity and ignore ability and economic identity. This is not about being politically correct; rather, it is about effectiveness in serving the community. You can't be all things to all people. Hopefully, there are other churches in your community that can fill the gaps that you can't fill, and vice versa. I am not saying that you shouldn't challenge yourself or your congregation. But don't say that you are going to serve the Native American community if there is not a Native American population within a hundred miles. Racial diversity is going to be easier in New York City, where racial and ethnic minorities are 65 percent of the population, than it will be in Boise, Idaho, where the white population is around 90 percent. If you are in San Antonio, where the Hispanic population is 64 percent, and your church is all white, then racial diversity is probably an issue you need to address. Ask the following questions:

- What are our goals for diversity, equity, and inclusion?

- Why are we doing this work?

- Are we committed to diversity and inclusion work?

- What types of resources are available to our leaders and members?

- How will we celebrate success?

3. *Get women involved.* According to a 2016 study, "the proportion of women in a training group was associated with more favorable reactions to diversity training."[4] Other studies show that women in general are more receptive to diversity and inclusion training. The activated church will have a place for women in leadership. If your theological leanings don't allow for women leaders, then this book probably is not for you. Maybe women are more empathetic, or maybe the historical marginalization of women gives them a greater perspective. Not only do women tend to be more receptive, but having women involved in organizational leadership has been shown to enhance decision-making by reducing groupthink, abuse, and fraud. According to a 2015 report about gender diversity on corporate boards, secular organizations with gender-diverse boards have fewer instances of controversial business practices such as fraud, corruption, bribery, and shareholder conflicts. "Companies lacking board diversity suffered more governance-related controversies than average."[5] If you are a male leader surrounded by a roomful of other male leaders, you are missing out on valuable wisdom that can be gained through diversity and inclusion.

4. *Get data.* Metrics matter, though many people in church frown on them. It is important to establish a baseline for your organization as well as to tie measurable outcomes to your goals. Several tools can assess where individuals are on a mindset and

personality level so that they and you are aware of their cultural capabilities and passions. Data empowers leaders to take steps to increase their cultural competency where necessary. One of the tools that I use as a qualified administrator is the Intercultural Development Inventory.

internet?

The Intercultural Development Inventory® (IDI®) assesses intercultural competence—the capability to shift cultural perspective and appropriately adapt behavior to cultural differences and commonalities. Intercultural competence has been identified as a critical capability in several studies focusing on effectiveness of international sojourners, international business adaptation and job performance, international student adjustment, international transfer of technology and information, international study abroad, and inter-ethnic relations within nations. IDI is a fifty-item questionnaire available online that can be completed in fifteen to twenty minutes.

5. *Get talking.* To reinforce an inclusive culture, churches must create spaces for dialogue, discussion, and disagreements. There must be spaces for dialogue both within individual groups and within the larger congregation. If individuals feel comfortable in raising viewpoints, congregations are more likely to create better solutions and gain important insights about issues before they snowball into larger unwieldy problems.

6. *Get started.* What is stopping you from getting started today? There is no time like the present to engage diversity and belonging by creating a culture of inclusion in your congregation. Contact the right expert and commit resources and time to the process.

In the gospel of Mark, Jesus says to the crowd and his disciples, "If any of you wants to be my follower, you must give up your own way, take up your cross, and follow me. If you try to hang on to your life, you will lose it. But if you give up your life for my sake and the sake of the Good News, you will save it.

And what do you benefit if you gain the whole world but lose your own soul?" (Mark 8:34-36 NLT). This ancient message is relevant for our institutional church today. I could paraphrase this Scripture by saying, "If we want to equip the body to follow Christ, we must give up our power. We must tear down our unhealthy cultural silos and follow Christ. If we try to hang on to what was, we will lose our way. But if we give over control to answer God's call, we have everything to gain." We have to be open to new people and new ways of doing things. I believe God's transforming power is available to all. We love and appreciate all of God's diverse creation without reservation, and when the day of judgment comes, we all must work out our salvation with careful consideration.

QUESTIONS FOR REFLECTION

1. How do you measure diversity in your context?

2. Are your diversity and inclusion goals reasonable based on your context?

3. Where can you improve as it relates to becoming a more diverse congregation?

4. Are you willing to change programs, leadership, and other aspects of your congregation to be more inclusive?

5. How does your leadership reflect the diversity you want to see in your church?

6. What are the top barriers to you becoming a more diverse and inclusive congregation?

7. Are there some theological barriers that you strategically adopted so as not to include certain groups of people?

8. Are there physical barriers that prevent access to your facilities and events?

SEVEN

Characteristic Five:
Holistic Witness to Serving the Community

> *At present, however, I am going to Jerusalem in a ministry to the saints; for Macedonia and Achaia have been pleased to share their resources with the poor among the saints at Jerusalem. They were pleased to do this, and indeed they owe it to them; for if the Gentiles have come to share in their spiritual blessings, they ought also to be of service to them in material things.*
> —ROMANS 15:25-27

WHEN I WAS a youth pastor, I took a group of students to Miami to participate in a short-term service program called DOOR, which takes volunteers to various city locations to serve. I learned two powerful lessons from that experience: First, regular superglue does not close self-inflicted knife wounds—it is not the same as the stuff used by doctors. Second, we must encounter our community through the eyes, ears, and heart of God. Seeing God in the city was an important part of the experience. Spending a week at DOOR transformed how I thought about ministry and engaging the community. Working outside of the church building and going to different locations to work alongside people and hearing their stories allowed me to experience ministry in a new way. The question that our group repeatedly asked ourselves was, "Where do you see God in the city?" God is not confined to our services or our boxed-in building. At the end of each workday, we reflected on that question and shared where we saw God that day. Often, we were tired and dirty after working. I am still haunted by the cold showers in the weird outside porta-potty-like shower contraptions. As the leader of the group, I had to deal with conflicts and logistical issues while coordinating the work. And at one point, in a rush to pack up supplies and tools so we could get the kids from one place to another, I stabbed myself with a knife. Thinking back on the experience settled in my mind that as we work in witness in the community, we must get our hands dirty, and maybe even bloodied. We might bleed a little as we are called to engage and lead.

Let me tell you why holistic witness is important. Hell on earth, or at least in America, is unfolding as I edit this book. We have a COVID-19 pandemic and homelessness, and unemployment is soaring. We have murder hornets; cities across the United States are on fire in response to incidents of racial injustice; and the president of the United States is waving a Bible in front of a burned-out church. Right before the president paused for that photo opportunity, U.S. military and civil police used tear gas and batons to clear peaceful protestors and ensure that the president was able to "do it for the 'gram." Breathe. As I type this outrageous description of events, the

Autobiography of Martin Luther King, Jr. sits at my left. The pages are open to Dr. King's description of the Watts riots of 1965. Some fifty-five years later, the cities are still burning because justice has failed to manifest itself. The church is being used as a prop for an Instagram photo rather than as a witness to God's peace. Dr. King said, "When people are voiceless, they will have temper tantrums like a little child who has not been paid attention to. And riots are massive temper tantrums from a neglected and voiceless people."[1] The activated church needs to lead the way in helping us to break the cycle of injustice.

Activated churches understand holistic witness in their respective context. André Gingerich Stoner, the former director of interchurch relations and holistic witness for Mennonite Church USA, describes such witness this way: "Holistic witness involves peacemaking and sharing faith; it involves helping birth new faith communities and seeking justice; it involves service and forgiveness. But these concerns are often pitted against each other."[2]

For the church to survive, the people must survive. Better yet, when the people thrive, the church thrives. Ministry is not limited to preaching and teaching Scripture—successful ministry emulates the holistic ministry example set by Christ. Many churches, either alone or as part of a network, are involved in the feeding and healing of the body through various programs. They are centers of social and political reform in the community. They often provide educational opportunities to help people climb the socioeconomic ladder, providing them with a sense of dignity. The activated church is also a refuge for the people when violence, disaster, and injustice infringe upon the community.

My interview with Pastor Misha, who is very involved in her community, illuminates the ministry of holistic witness. I wanted to know why her congregation was so engaged in what folks might think of as activism. She shared, "I like to think it's an extension of the gospel, how we interpret the Gospels. As far as our congregation, I don't think it would make sense to have a congregational life that, in some way, did not extend to people outside the walls of our church. It feels embedded in who we are. This was the spirit of the church, even before I became the pastor. Now it seems we moved a little bit deeper into how we engage the community. We are now thinking about systemic issues more than simply looking at involvement in the community, like feeding the hungry. Now we want to ask why problems exist in the community, and what are the unmet needs."

Pastor Misha went on to share some of the questions asked by members of her congregation: "Why do we have homelessness? Why are there women in prison? How are all these things interconnected?" She continued, "We try to see what forms of power are at work in our community. We want to see if things can change by our church addressing that power. We may look to join coalitions of people who help us to think about ways change can happen. Then together with those coalitions, we can act." The church can be part of the power of change in a community, especially as it comes to issues of justice. The secular society may value the power of the church more than the church itself values our ability to facilitate transformation. Why do I say this?

Look at politicians, the lawmakers in this country. The first stop on the campaign trail is often at a local congregation. Campaign staff know the value of connecting with prominent religious community leaders. These leaders pat the politicians on the back, essentially endorsing them before the congregation. Various presidents have used religion to one degree or another to connect with their base. Although we have separation of church and state in America, the state realizes the historical importance and influence of the church in the community, although that influence may well be waning in the younger generations. Pastor Misha, a millennial pastor, still understands the power the church has and that living into holistic witness means using that power to speak to the power of injustice.

Pastor Misha and her congregation live into the symbiotic nature of the community. They intentionally do not own the building in which they worship. She explained, "We've never owned a building, and it really is in our DNA not to own a building. In some way, that makes us feel more connected; we need the community, and we are dependent upon others to offer space for us. So when we worship, it is not like, oh, it's us in here, and we have our building. We can't just shut the doors and have our Bible studies. We are sharing space with the community, so we are vulnerable. We depend on the hospitality of other people. It's been like this from the beginning, so it shapes us. We must set up our chairs every week. We need to lay out our hymnals. And our walls are decorated with superhero posters because we meet in a school. So we kind of started from doing church this way in the very beginning. It makes us think about being local in ways that other churches might not have to consider."

I appreciate the unique attitude of Pastor Misha's church. That is why it's so important for us to understand our identity as congregations. We must know and understand the community that we are called to be a part of so that we can meet the needs of that community. I appreciate the fact that this church, which is in North Carolina, doesn't have a building. When we are locked away in our pristine ivory towers, it is easy for us to ignore the world. The church works best when we need each other, when we can depend on each other, and when there is mutual support and a mutual exchange of gifts. I often wonder if buildings and sprawling complexes are actually barriers to the church being able to share the gospel effectively. I often warn young pastors about the dangers of planting a building, rather than planting a church. Developing the lives of people and strengthening the community of believers is much more important than the prestige of signing a lease or owning the place where you meet. Too many church planters start with the physical location in mind, rather than understanding that the people are the strongest foundation you can build. Once we get into the real estate business, we lose focus on sharing the gospel. Our time is consumed with paying the rent and the electric bill. With a building, the pastor spends a great deal of time making ends meet versus helping people meet their spiritual needs. Again, the physical distancing and inability to meet in person required in response to the COVID-19 pandemic taught many of us clergy that we can do church without a physical building. Anecdotal evidence reported from my denominational leaders suggests that churches can serve people in deep and meaningful ways without having a huge facility. Not that I am against building ownership, but facilities should not drive the mission.

One thing the activated church can be is a place of healing for people turned off by other churches or for people who have been hurt by ministries that focused on other priorities. Pastor Misha sees her small congregation as a place of healing. She said, "I appreciate that our church is sort of like a hospital for people recovering from really painful and often violent forms of Christianity. Recovery also can be for LGBTQIA+ people; this can be people who just grew up in very fundamentalist traditions. We are a Mennonite church, and that is in our name. So we aren't going to draw big crowds. Maybe you have to be a little weird to walk into a Mennonite church in North Carolina. There's already something about people who come to our church. They are not looking for tradition, and they are bringing their whole self to the door. They know that things are not as they ought to be, and they are open to healing. This kind of healing doesn't just happen in our limited congregational life. It is something that also involves healing outside of our congregational life."

As I continued my conversation with Pastor Misha, I was amused as she talked about the unchurched people she was attracting and the unintended church growth her congregation was experiencing. For someone who did not believe in the so-called "seeker-friendly movement," the fruit of her work seemed very friendly to folks seeking answers. As I think about the principles outlined in chapter 2, I notice that Pastor Misha engaged and connected with people effectively using many SEO principles. Pastor Misha and her church understand that effectively engaging the community does not mean that you become just another social club or that you must water down the gospel. I asked her about attracting unchurched folks.

"Do we have a lot of unchurched? Yes, and people that have not been to church in a long time. You're always told in seminary that you're supposed to be doing ministry to the unchurched, but it never actually happened to me before. It's very surprising to find that we are attracting so many unchurched people and figuring out what it means. As a minister, I started to just think about how we articulate what we were doing in the community. We are not just being nice and doing charity. Folks are not coming to our church because we are another club. For people who join us, groups like the Rotary Club or Habitat for Humanity were not enough. We don't just want to be another place for service projects. We want to present a more radical vision. When people come to us, we challenge them on what it means for us to do life together and how that might involve other people, the community."

Again, as I talk to pastors and leaders on the move, it is clear that to reach millennial and younger generations, to be connected beyond the clique of people raised in the church, we must send the message that there is a cause worth dying for and that we all have a purpose worthy of living.

Too often, the church and other institutions like it become so inward-looking that they only exist to serve themselves. The institution becomes the core we try to preserve. We are willing to protect the institution above the integrity of the community. Churches, at times, have become selfish. They fight to survive in times of crisis rather than creating a system in which they and the community can thrive.

When the pandemic hit and the entire world shut down, countries like Italy, South Korea, Brazil, and China were just a few of the nations trying to keep the coronavirus from spreading. Even the United States had to mobilize various corporations to keep up with demand for medical supplies. For a time, the entire country shut down. We closed schools and parks, and most concerts and major sporting events were postponed or canceled. There was fear and confusion in the United States and across the world.

As I wrote this book and watched our world change, I saw that people were fearful of losing their jobs, losing their homes, and losing their lives. At times I was not too impressed with the ways that many in the church responded. A couple of trends emerged. Some churches called for prayer, telling people not to panic, and speaking words of hope. That's a good thing. There were lots of thoughts and prayers being shared. But a dangerous trend also emerged amid this global pandemic. Many churches were trying to figure out what was going to happen with Sunday's offering. I heard calls from pastors saying, "Have faith, believe that God will overcome this disease," but I heard the fear as I listened beyond the actual words. The fear said, "If folks don't show up for church on Sunday, we won't get our tithes and offerings. How will my church survive?" Amid a crisis, the church should be a giver; after all, we are not a consumer-based business. We receive tax breaks, and we receive offerings week after week. If anyone should be prepared to weather an economic crisis, it should be the church.

Look at the story of Joseph as he guided Egypt through a famine. "[Joseph] gathered up all the food of the seven years when there was plenty in the land of Egypt, and stored up food in the cities; he stored up in every city the food from the fields around it. . . . And the seven years of famine began to come, just as Joseph had said. . . . And since the famine had spread over all the land, Joseph opened all the storehouses and sold to the Egyptians, for the famine was severe in the land of Egypt. Moreover, all the world came to Joseph in Egypt to buy grain" (Genesis 41:48, 54, 56-57). Joseph was a man touched by God. God spoke to Joseph, and because Joseph listened, he was able to provide for his community and others during the midst of a great famine. Wouldn't it be wonderful if the church of today could do the same in its communities instead of worrying if a crisis was going to cause us to lose out on tithes and offerings? What if this global pandemic was an opportunity for the global church to shine by providing resources, stability, and peace in the middle of chaos? Thankfully, many churches did respond and help the community; those are the activated churches.

Some churches fell into the political polarities of the moment. The decision of whether to open a church for worship became more about political affiliation and less about taking care of the community in some cases. (While I did not want to spend too much time on COVID-19 and detract from the overall theme of this book, I did think it would be helpful to include a resource on responding to crises. Check it out in the back of this book when you have time. Sadly, the high-profile killings of several Black men and women at the hands of police and white vigilantes made 2020 seemed like one never-ending crisis.) Political polarities and issues of justice are not new to the church. Without being trapped in romanticizing the past, we must learn from past missteps of the church. How did the church react in other times of polarization surrounding justice and holistic witness? Factions of the church often circle the wagon depending on how an issue hits them personally. We need to stop that horrific practice and be more empathetic. The lesson I learned from Pastor Misha is that the church needs to analyze the power it has, see the power disparities in its community, and then use its power to fight for equity, for justice. That is holistic witness in action.

During the civil rights movement, Christian pastor Martin Luther King Jr. and Muslim leader Malcolm X were both labeled "God's angry men." They understood the power of the church to bring about change even in the disenfranchised Black community. They both challenged, though in drastically different ways, the white institution, the white church, to step up and join the fight. I mention both Malcolm X and Dr. King as an illustration of contrasts. Both religious leaders stepped out to fight the same injustice, but in very different ways. Dr. King and others put themselves in great peril fighting for justice, moving the church beyond worship, but also fighting for the vulnerable. There is a symbiosis to the relationship between Dr. King and Malcom X that I won't address here, but I know both men understood one another. One had the philosophy of turning the other cheek. The other had a philosophy of "by any means necessary." The cause was greater than the congregation or even one local community. How much is the church of today willing to risk? How much are you willing to risk as a leader to do what is right?

Tragically, both were assassinated fighting for justice. Martin Luther King Jr. wrote his "Letter from Birmingham Jail" in response to criticism of nonviolent protests in Birmingham, Alabama, in April 1963. Dr. King responded specifically to a statement published in a local newspaper by eight white clergy calling the civil rights protests "unwise and untimely" and condemning the "outsiders" who led the protests. Dr. King argued that he was in Birmingham "because injustice is here," and like the apostle Paul and other early Christians, he had to answer the call for aid or, as I would say, holistic witness.

Look, let me honest. I am not trying to die. Not soon, anyway. Dying is something you can only do once, and once you fall on your sword, that is it. I believe in taking risks, but I also weigh the risks I take as a leader. I know where God has placed my passion, and I know the areas of justice where I can be the most and the least effective. I have a deep understanding of what peacemaking and justice mean to me. I also know that I have gaps in my understanding. Daily, I work to be more compassionate and to learn how to love more like Jesus.

André Gingerich Stoner shared,

> If we take the whole Jesus seriously, I think our witness will also involve peacemaking, service, justice-seeking, and evangelism. And it will be both pastoral and prophetic.
>
> It would be worthwhile [to unpack] further what we mean by prophetic. I think it involves speaking the truth; it involves addressing structures and systems. And it can involve risk and conflict. I think sometimes, however, we make being "prophetic" synonymous with being shrill and harsh. The way of the cross holds together deep love and compassion with a bold challenge to sin, injustice, and evil. That is the invitation for all who would put on the mind of Christ.[3]

The activated church and its leaders have to ask ourselves, Where do we see God in others, and if we aren't seeing that hope that comes from the presence of God, what barriers need to be dismantled?

QUESTIONS FOR REFLECTION

1. What are the challenges in your community for which your church can help provide solutions?

2. Are you able to determine the root causes of these challenges?

3. What challenges are your members most passionate about or best equipped to address?

4. Rather than starting from scratch, what are the coalitions or movements your congregation can be a part of to enhance the work?

5. How can you speak to or otherwise influence the government or those in power on behalf of those who are powerless?

6. Where do you see God in your community?

7. What are you willing to risk?

EIGHT

Characteristic Six:
Developing Strategic Partnerships

> *"Teacher, which commandment in the law is the*
> *greatest?" He said to him, "'You shall love the Lord*
> *your God with all your heart, and with all your soul,*
> *and with all your mind.' This is the greatest and first*
> *commandment. And a second is like it: 'You shall love*
> *your neighbor as yourself.' On these two commandments*
> *hang all the law and the prophets."*
> —MATTHEW 22:36-40

A STRATEGIC PARTNERSHIP describes a working relationship between two organizations as they link arms to provide encouragement, relational power, and resources within a clearly defined set of principles, goals, and values. Strategic partnerships bring together often diverse groups in the fulfillment of a shared vision. For the activated church, strategic partnerships can be bridges that build important relationships, allowing the church to be a loving neighbor while fostering health, well-being, and healing for those outside the congregation.

I recently had a conversation with a church planter/campus missionary friend of mine. Our kids went to the same school, and Minister Chuck has been involved with several different ministry projects, including church administration and working for Campus Crusade for Christ (now known as Cru). I was interested in how he decided which movements and organizations he would be a part of and what his philosophy of ministry is. For Chuck, it all starts with the great commandment found in Matthew 22:36-40.

When selecting strategic partnerships to get involved with as part of his ministry, Chuck believes that the values of the partner need to line up with the great commandment. "Are the community efforts you are connecting with helping you to love yourself and to love your neighbor? When I think about a church, I define church as a gathering of believers, and believers grow best in the context of a loving Christian community," he said. Chuck and his team are starting with dispersed community groups in various locations. Some leaders will begin their work in schools, and some in homes and even in a local gymnasium. The goal is to build the church from the outside in and not the other way around.

According to Chuck, the Western church attendee has assumed a posture that reflects the question, "What have you done for me lately?" Chuck and his team want to remind us that we are "not the individual finger of Christ," pointing to what we individually desire. We are "the body of Christ, a part of the whole," community together to serve one another and to hold each other accountable. Chuck thinks strategic community partnerships should be about health, well-being, and healing to the whole, much like the model of the early church in Acts.

Now the whole group of those who believed were of one heart and soul, and no one claimed private ownership of any possessions, but everything they owned was held in common. With great power the apostles gave their testimony to the resurrection of the Lord Jesus, and great grace was upon them all. There was not a needy person among them, for as many as owned lands or houses sold them and brought the proceeds of what was sold. They laid it at the apostles' feet, and it was distributed to each as any had need. (Acts 4:32-35)

One key difference is that beyond the church of today, there are many governmental, civic, and corporate organizations that provide for urgent needs in the local community. Rather than starting from scratch, Chuck recommends partnering with these groups even if they are not specifically Christian. Church leaders might ask, "How do you partner with a group without appearing that you are endorsing a particular lifestyle?" You must use wisdom when looking at partners, Christian or otherwise. There are times to walk alongside organizations that are fulfilling a Christlike mission, even if Christ is not the foundation of their organizational mission. "Feeding the hungry is the right thing to do, so I am willing to partner with groups that feed the hungry even if their identity is not specifically Christian," said Chuck. This is not to say that the church should not engage in discernment when forming partnerships. If the primary identity of the group is at odds with who you say you are as a Christian or a ministry, it is probably best not to partner with that group. The key question to ask when connecting with strategic partners is, Are the things they are doing aligning with the teaching of Christ?

As we think about community partnerships, those relationships can happen in several ways:

- We can open our space to established community programs.
- We can create programs in our space.

- We can go offsite and provide volunteers to the community.
- We can develop crisis-activated teams that join a cadre of other community volunteers.
- We can regularly fund various programs.

Community space. While I have cautioned against buildings, I am not anti–church property. Our space must serve the mission of the church. Space is probably the greatest asset that we have as individual congregations today. Most churches only have worship twice a week—a Sunday service and a midweek service. What are we doing with our space for the rest of the week? While sharing space is not the only way we can facilitate community partnerships, we should not undervalue the potential of our real estate for community engagement. If we own space, we need to think creatively about its use. Our real estate usually has three major components: interior structure, outdoor green space, and other exterior space, which is typically parking. All three components can be used in important ways to have an impact on the community.

Community playgrounds. If your church has a positive impact on the surrounding community and wants to nourish bodies as well as souls, providing a safe place for children to play is a great way to use your green space. Numerous organizations provide grants to help offset the cost of building community playgrounds. Groups like KABOOM!, General Mills, and American Parks Company are just a few organizations or companies that award grants for playgrounds. Do your research to see what is available in your area. PlayCore is one company that has curated a comprehensive funding guide that identifies grant opportunities that begin at the local community level, all the way to cities, states, and internationally.[1]

After-school programs. Affordable after-school programs can assist parents and communities in providing children activities, tutoring, and childcare during the hours of the day that have been deemed the most dangerous time for children. Many churches also use after-school programs to generate income. Churches can outsource the management of these programs. Depending on the community, children need places that will occupy their time with meaningful experiences to prevent them from getting involved in gangs or violence or other kinds of trouble. After-school programs can also be beneficial in ensuring children have access to the Internet for educational purposes and to healthy meals. Of all the partnership opportunities, after-school programs are probably the most demanding of time and facility use. There may be grants available for meals, educational equipment, program fees, and playground equipment.

Job and life skills programs. Dr. Martin Luther King Jr. was a leader who understood the impact of poverty on the community. In his book *Where Do We Go from Here: Chaos or Community?*, Dr. King writes, "The time has come for us to civilize ourselves by the total, direct and immediate abolition of poverty."[2] As churches, we need to not only help people who currently live in poverty, but also provide solutions to help them get out of or avoid poverty. There are many programs across the United States that offer job and life skills training. Churches can offer these programs space to meet and volunteers to teach, mentor, and counsel people in need. The church can also promote these programs and educate people on how to access these resources. Transportation to these programs is often a barrier. Churches can provide solutions to increase access.

Music and arts education programs. Music education is a great way to serve the community and potentially strengthen your worship experience. Many public schools face budget cuts and are eliminating their arts programs. Churches can help fill the gap by offering programs while also inviting participants to share their skills as part of the congregational worship experience. The programs can also expose members to Scripture and worship traditions in a more appealing way.

Local radio stations. Radio stations often host live events that bring the community together. Not only can you help the radio station, but you can create greater exposure for your congregation and ministry programs. Many radio stations also run community announcements at little or no charge. Get the message out to the community you care about, and you are engaged as a church.

Creative community events. Churches can host events or provide volunteers for community events. There are many creative opportunities for church engagement. Instead of bringing people to your campus, go out into the community. Some sports venues provide opportunities for nonprofits to staff concessions or parking. Seasonal festivals allow nonprofits to set up booths. Check your community calendar to see what is planned and where you can engage.

Garden and urban farming programs. Local and urban farming initiatives can have a profound impact on the health and well-being of the community. These gardens bring volunteers and community members together to collaborate, learn, and meet needs. A lack of access to fresh, healthy foods can contribute to poor diets, obesity, and many diet-related diseases. Gardens can have a positive lasting impact on the community, especially in areas designated as "food deserts"—communities with poor access to supermarkets and healthier foods.

Food pantry. A food pantry program collects and stores food and household products for free distribution to people in need. Before you begin planning your own food pantry, contact your local food bank to see what the needs are. Again, you may be better able to help meet the need in your community by joining forces with an existing program than by duplicating services within the area. Local food banks often need volunteers to help with sorting and distribution. Your ministry could also become a satellite location that enhances the network of food availability.

Crisis response ministry. Does your county, state, or local township have a crisis response ministry? There are nondenominational organizations that instruct you and your ministry team on how to provide physical, emotional, and spiritual support during times of crisis. This is one way to coordinate with other faith-based groups in your community. Some programs will allow your team to be "certified," and that will seamlessly allow you to collaborate and coordinate with other crisis and disaster-focused volunteer organizations. Establishing a partnership with these organizations can streamline the process of getting needed aid to church members.

Recovery organizations. There are probably many successful recovery organizations already in existence in your community, but they need safe spaces to meet. Adding a faith component or connection can be a source of hope and healing to people isolated by addiction. According to *Psychology Today*, "Spiritual growth involves a connection to people, the world, and a higher purpose than oneself. It also may embody values like trust, faith, respect, self-expression, and self-acceptance. These are exactly the things that are needed in the lives of many an addicted person who may be struggling with self-loathing and isolation."[3] Church partnerships solidify an important spiritual foundation for the treatment those in recovery receive.

Local schools. Believe it or not, churches can legally partner with schools. There are many ways for churches to do so. Schools are important centers of activity in our communities. Public schools are one of the institutions that bring together the full diversity of the community. They influence people of all ages and backgrounds. The strength of the schools even goes beyond parents. Multiple generations are connected through school engagement. People are highly invested in the health of community schools. Even if people do not have students in the schools, the schools can affect property values and employment opportunities as well. Here are a few tips when seeking to partner with schools:

- Be mindful of respecting the laws separating church and state.

- Take the time to understand the needs of the school. Come ready to serve. It is best to have honest discussions about the resources needed for the partnership to be successful.

- Be pragmatic about the resources that each partner is realistically able to contribute to the collaboration.

- Cultivate multiple relationships with staff and key administrators. A lot of transition may happen in public schools.

- Focus on both short-term and long-term student achievement.

Local law enforcement. Many in the Black community cannot disassociate policing from its historical roots. As professor Victor Kappeler writes, "The birth and development of the American police can be traced to a multitude of historical, legal, and political-economic conditions. The institution of slavery and the control of minorities, however, were two of the more formidable historic features of American society shaping early policing. Slave patrols and Night Watches, which later became modern police departments, were both designed to control the behaviors of minorities."[4] The relationship between the community and law enforcement is going to be a top justice issue over the next few years. There are many cries to defund the police or significantly reform law enforcement. Meaningful change takes time. The church needs to be a part of that change and must not ignore the diversity of thought and the diversity of experiences when it comes to how police are perceived. As people seek reform, there will be plenty of opportunities for the Christian community to build bridges and offer support. Churches can also facilitate conversations between the police and the community, educating community members on how they can be actively involved in community problem-solving. Having connections with law enforcement can provide a great source of information for members. Congregations can host meetings and other activities that build trust between the police and those they serve. Partnering with law enforcement leads to the empowerment of the community. The ability of communities to convey their concerns to the police and to become partners in finding solutions to their problems can lead to improved crime prevention and safety and an enhanced perception of security.

Partnerships between the police and the church allow for radical discipleship. That being said, the church must always be mindful of its distinction from the state. The church must remember its unique position as the body of Christ and not an extension of any political agenda. We must resist the tendency to trust law enforcement without nuance; that is, to trust the police implicitly and to distrust voices that may be critical of or mindful of complicating truths, historic racism, and cultural differences. Radical discipleship is about responding to God's gracious call in Christ and putting faith into action, especially when it comes to confronting violence, poverty, and other actions connected to injustice.

Federal programs. Even the federal government recognizes the importance of faith-based communities. There have been several executive orders by recent presidents to promote strategic partnerships between congregations and the community. The White House issued the following order a few years ago:

Faith-based and community organizations have tremendous ability to serve individuals, families, and communities through means that are different from those of government and with capacity that often exceeds that of government. These organizations lift people, keep families strong, and solve problems at the local level. The executive branch wants faith-based and community organizations, to the fullest opportunity permitted by law, to compete on a level playing field for grants, contracts, programs, and other federal funding opportunities. The efforts of faith-based and community organizations are essential to revitalizing communities, and the federal government welcomes opportunities to partner with such organizations through innovative, measurable, and outcome-driven initiatives.[5]

As the executive order communicates, churches can apply for these grants.

Whatever partnership your congregation decides to undertake, you must know how it affects your outward-facing strategy. In their outward strategy, Minister Chuck and his team identify the following goals:

- Help people encounter God.
- Disciple followers.
- Equip leaders.
- Send leaders.

Helping people encounter God can happen in any number of ways. Every encounter or every partnership may not lead to growing your church. Sometimes we just need to be the church. More members should not always be the goal. More engagement can be a goal. Engagement is creating more and more pathways to strengthen relationships or understanding.

Chuck and his team are not trying to hoard bodies. They are intentional, not to grow a megachurch but to equip people to be the church and connect with people where they are. The church should be a place of equipping and sending, not of hoarding resources, gifts, and talents. In some sense, the Western church has become too consumer-minded. Churches are gearing themselves to be one-stop shops like Wal-Mart or shopping malls, isolated from the rest of the community. When the church is connected to the community, it works alongside other groups. It weaves its mission into serving and shares what it has broadly. A theme that Henry Blackaby and Claude King emphasize in their book *Experiencing God* is to "find out where God is working and join Him." In our arrogance as church leaders, we go straight to asking God to bless our vision instead of taking time to pray and listen to see what God's vision is and then join it. Our first and primary strategic partnership should be acknowledging and connecting to the move of the Spirit. "When the Spirit of truth comes, he will guide you into all truth. He will not speak on his own but will tell you what he has heard. He will tell you about the future. He will bring me glory by telling you whatever he receives from me" (John 16:13-14 NLT).

Chuck calls this walking with Jesus and walking out Jesus' commandments. Jesus was very countercultural. God did not see fit to stay separate from humans or to do the work of transformation through the established religious bureaucracy. God sent Jesus to earth to walk among the people, to be part of the community, and to touch the lives of people in need. The power of God was manifested not so much in the temple as it was in towns, homes, and places of business. As people of the New Testament, we need to realize that the power of the Spirit is no longer contained in a box or a building. The power of the Spirit has been unleashed to transform lives throughout the community. As the church, we must trust that it is the Spirit of God who is the transformer, and that our strategic partnerships are the ways we connect to the movement of God. We harness and cultivate the fruit of that transformation to live out the great commandment.

One size often does not fit all the needs of our community members. In times of crisis, there is little time to focus on the numerous differences between groups. To quote from *Star Trek*, "The needs of the many outweigh the [selfish desires] of the few." To quote from Scripture, "The harvest is plentiful, but the laborers are few" (Matthew 9:37; Luke 10:2). Meeting great needs takes some great partners and a strong network of churches all working together: Anabaptists, evangelicals, independents, and others. One organization that helps churches with strategic partnerships is the Christian Community Development Association. In their messaging, they share, "The church must be involved in every aspect of a person's life. It is important to network with other churches and organizations in communities. To accomplish the wholistic aspect of ministry, pastors and leaders must be networkers. Christian Community Development builds coalitions in communities so that they can work together to solve the problems."[6] Albeit with some variation, CCDA's philosophy focuses on principles that very much align with characteristics of the activated church. If you are interested in tools and training to strengthen your capacity in the area of strategic community partnerships, I encourage you to visit their website (ccda.org) and check out their eight-point philosophy.

The culture and ethnic identity of your congregation may play an important role in what community partnerships look like, especially when it comes to the issue of social justice. The African American church has tended to have a strong relationship with the local community. The Black church was at the forefront of the civil rights movement. This is highlighted in the article "Pulpits and Platforms: The Role of the Church in Determining Protest among Black Americans": "Despite the fact that some formal church leaders were slow to support civil rights activism, the black church facilitated activism in at least two important ways. First, as evidenced by the speeches of the Rev. Martin Luther King, Jr., religious themes and biblical references were central to the framing of the Civil Rights movement. Second, the churches played a key role in the mobilization of blacks by providing the organizational and institutional resources necessary for boycotts, sit-ins, and other protest activities. Churches are also a mechanism for pooling and organizing resources."[7] Notably, while trends show declines in church participation, according to a 2014 study, Black millennials still tend to be more religious than other groups.[8] The trend highlights a very important point for churches who wish to attract young people and speak to their areas of concern: diversity and inclusion matter and community engagement matters.

As churches, we need to give up the desire to control everything. We should not have our heads buried so deeply in the sand that we miss the good work already taking place around us. Churches alone can't meet all the needs in our communities. There are people in our towns and cities who are already doing life-giving work daily. Good stewardship means that the activated church leader is out in the local community, uncovering ways to partner with other great organizations and events already in action. Community partnerships are about multiplication. If we work together across the usual divisions, the Spirit can work through us and expand our reach beyond the limited capabilities of individual houses of worship.

QUESTIONS FOR REFLECTION

1. What are the most urgent needs in your community?

2. Who is addressing those needs and doing it well?

3. Who are the key influencers in your community with whom you need to connect?

4. Where does your target audience gather most frequently?

5. Is your church equipped to go out into the community, or are you positioned so people have easy access to you?

6. Do your ministry programs articulate a cause worth dying for and a life-giving mission?

NINE

Characteristic Seven:
Practicing Sound Stewardship

Now the whole group of those who believed were of one heart and soul, and no one claimed private ownership of any possessions, but everything they owned was held in common. . . . There was not a needy person among them, for as many as owned lands or houses sold them and brought the proceeds of what was sold. They laid it at the apostles' feet, and it was distributed to each as any had need.

—ACTS 4:32, 34-35

I ONCE READ that "stewardship is a role, giving is an act, and generosity is an attitude."[1] It made me think of the parable of the unjust steward in Luke 16:1-13. A steward is a person who manages the resources of another. The steward in this parable had authority over the master's resources and could transact business in the master's name. The master held the utmost level of trust in the steward. I have found this parable a little troubling at times; even scholars disagree on its meaning. I will let the theologians fight it out to determine the meaning, but I notice that the steward was wise enough to understand what the money represented to his master. Sure, you might think the steward was somewhat wicked. He was bad at his job and only escaped persecution by falsifying documents. The scheme worked because everyone in the system was dishonest, and the boss was a bad record-keeper. In the end, the lesson I've taken from this parable is to be smart when it comes to managing my affairs and to operate with integrity because corruption begets corruption. In more colloquial terms, the lesson of the parable might be "Don't get caught up"—manage your affairs with wisdom, especially when managing someone else's stuff. The church has a responsibility to manage its resources with expertise and integrity. This parable is also an illustration of the challenges Christians have with money. Other than human sexuality, money is one of the most divisive topics in church, but we all need the value it represents to accomplish our goals.

Today, we have what is called fiat money. Fiat money is government-issued currency that is backed not by any type of physical commodity, such as gold or silver, but rather by the government that issued it. The value of fiat money is derived from the relationship between supply and demand. It is also based on the stability of the issuing government. It is just a promise. Transferring fiat money is an act of faith. If I give you X amount of this paper, you will do B or give me C in return. Money represents three things: (1) time (labor to earn it), (2) power (control), and (3) faith (a promise to deliver value). The church needs to stop thinking about the currency itself as good or evil and to instead consider these three representations.

STEWARDSHIP

Good stewardship leads to the activated church thinking of money as a tool to help people manage their time and talents, mitigate abuses of power, and exercise faith in a way that lines up with God's Word. That's it. Money isn't magic; it isn't a demon. Having money is not something that should lead one to shame. Money is a tool. Successfully activated churches have sound stewardship practices and knowledge. I love it when churches can teach about money and educate members to have a healthy relationship with money versus being a slave to our culture's materialism. Good leaders understand how to manage money, and they inspire good stewardship in the community. The successful church and its leaders establish sound financial practices, operate with a measure of faith, and teach the principle of sowing and reaping. Every farmer knows that you have to plant seed in the ground before the vegetables appear. You have to take care of the soil, fertilize the ground, water the seed, and then—boom!—corn, cabbages, or rutabagas pop up. It's not magic, it's hard work. It's a practical earthly principle and a bit of God's grace in the form of the weather. Finances work along the same lines.

The church can help its members in practical living and education about how to manage personal finances, moving people in the community from a mentality of poverty and consumerism to one where needs are met with generosity. Successful churches can thrive even in an impoverished context because transformation begins in the minds of the people. "Don't copy the behavior and customs of this world, but let God transform you into a new person by changing the way you think. Then you will learn to know God's will for you, which is good and pleasing and perfect" (Romans 12:2 NLT). A church that practices and teaches sound stewardship helps us think differently about how we use money. Money and personal resources shift from a source for personal gain to a tool to share with and bless the entire community.

Churches need to calculate the cost of ministry and plan for it. Good stewardship is about the management of the blessings God provides. Stewardship is as much about faithful practices as it is about having faith. Too many churches are surviving Sunday to Sunday because their planning exceeds their offering. What does it say to members about the management of their finances if the church can't effectively manage its own? I keep going back to the story of Joseph in Egypt. As I noted earlier, because Joseph listened to what he heard from God, he was able to provide for his community and others during a great famine. Joseph was an excellent steward. Not only did he depend on his faith, but he executed the faith through some pretty high-level accounting and resource management.

It breaks my heart to read or hear story after story about the tough decisions churches had to make during natural disasters and other times of crisis. Many small churches have to ask, "Do we open because we need tithes and offerings, or do we stay closed to protect the health, safety, and well-being of our members?" My vote would be for the health and well-being of my members. Sadly, I am not just talking about the COVID-19 pandemic. I have heard this same question asked during floods, hurricanes, and other risky situations. Pastors have joked, "I can't shut down on a Sunday. I need this month." These conversations are far too common. An article in *Christianity Today* reports, "Social scientist of religion Cleve V. Tinsley IV says that '[t]here are multiple reasons these large mega-churches may keep their doors open, reasons that relate to a complex web of fear of paying large mortgages and staff salaries, smaller Black churches collapsing because of lack of institutional and financial support; they also may not have the kind of larger structural resources to maintain their buildings that some mainline churches have when their doors close and giving in-evitably drops off.'"[2] As they say in my hometown, "Houston, we have a problem."[3] The church needs to practice stewardship and be an example to the community. Money should never trump the safety and well-being of the people in the pew. We are there to serve them, not the other way around.

POWER

Reflecting on my conversation with Pastor Misha, whose church I introduced in my earlier discussion about serving the community, I noticed that her congregation approaches giving in a different way, one which strongly reflects their mission and their theology. An important part of their work that connects community engagement with stewardship is paying attention to the economic situation of young adults and the increasing role that debt plays in their lives. Her congregation buys back people's loans. The member then sets up a 0 percent payback plan with the church. Pastor Misha said, "This is our way of fighting what we believe is a satanic predatory system." The work the church does is not only debt relief but education. "We had one member who ended up with this medical debt," shared Pastor Misha. "He didn't realize—because many of us don't know anything about the debt system—he didn't realize he could get this written off or at least set up a payment plan. So he panicked, and he took out a credit card loan to pay for the medical debt. It just creates this debt death cycle."

As we think about the role of the church when it comes to stewardship, it's not only managing the resources that we are given, but also taking a deeper look at the economic situation of our members. The activated church, once again, must be in tune with the needs of its members. Hopefully, our church-es have broad economic diversity; if they don't, then those churches that are more privileged should help those that are underprivileged. I think that is essential to the community and to being a good steward of our resources. That is why it is imperative that as we think about soliciting tithes and offerings from our members, which I do think is necessary, we need to understand how that affects the community within and outside our walls. We must prayerfully consider what we are doing with those resources once we solicit them. Are we using those resources to better the community and the people who we connect with, or are we using those finances to build bright, shining edifices?

Pastor Misha put it this way: "I think being serious about economic division, actually putting that on the table to have a real conversation about what that means generationally and how it impacts our neighborhoods, is essential. Gentrification in our neighborhoods needs to be part of the discussion. We just had a couple in our congregation moved into a gentrifying neighborhood. This was a neighborhood that the wife's family had been kicked out of. She watched friends and neighbors slowly get pushed out of the neighborhood." Part of the ministry of the church was helping this couple think through what the economic reality meant for them and their faith walk. They helped the couple wrestle with their financial strategy and how that connected to their faith walk as Christians. Pastor Misha closed by saying, "I think that couple is going to leave that neighborhood because now they know what it means for people to be in community and how divisive it can be when society pits the haves against the have-nots."

GENEROSITY

I recently gave away a car. It was nothing fancy, but it ran, and the air conditioning blew ice-cold. You can't ask for anything more in the hundred-degree Texas heat. But I didn't need it, and I wasn't interested in selling it for the few hundred bucks it would net me. To be a hundred percent honest, I didn't want the hassle of selling it.

It is the third vehicle my wife and I have given away. A long time ago, somewhere along the path of our journey together, we decided that selling stuff we no longer needed was not going to be our modus operandi. For us, our time could be better spent elsewhere than setting up a yard sale and sorting out dollars and cents. We know we have too much stuff, and we know that we are blessed, so as we transition or replace items, we try very hard to give them away to people who want or need them. Early in our life, when we had less material wealth, people gave generously to us. In a sense, we are paying it forward.

One thing about free stuff is that the price is always right if given in the spirit of generosity. I don't give away junk. I don't give away anything that I don't value. Two decades ago, when my first child was born, a family friend decided to pass down some very nice and fashionable clothes that her daughter had outgrown. Each school year, we got a batch of new clothes from this friend. Our friend loved shopping, and we loved receiving. The price—free—was right, and we didn't have to buy our daughter much clothing for the first five or six years of her life. This generosity was not rare in my church. My pastor gave us furniture, neckties, and even helped us with the earnest money payment for our first home. It was such a blessing to be part of a church community that was so generous.

The culture of generosity was strong in this African American faith community. Shockingly, many think that communities of color are always needy, are always looking for a handout, or need an outside white savior to lift them up. My African American Anabaptist faith community was not like that at all. From the pulpit and the pew we were taught, and we practiced, generosity. A high percentage of members were faithful tithers. We talked about money, and we shared our material possessions. I sincerely believe the spirit of generosity has paid dividends in the life of my family and the people in our sphere of influence. We have always had enough, even when times were tight. When you are generous with others, and when you are also a gracious receiver of generosity, you know you will have a safety net in your life.

One underestimated aspect of generosity is being a gracious receiver. When someone offers to give me a financial or other kind of blessing, I always accept it. I don't do the whole false humility thing—"Oh, no, I couldn't," or "You shouldn't have." I say, "Thank you so much. I really appreciate your generosity." Why do I do that? Well, for one reason, I say to myself, "Who am I to cut off someone's blessing?" The Lord may have told that person to make a personal sacrifice. That person may need to practice the discipline of reaping and sowing. That person may just need to perform an act of kindness to help him or herself through something. Why would I dishonor them with false humility when I could be igniting the fire of generosity? In Acts 4, we see the early church practicing generosity: "Now the whole group of those who believed were of one heart and soul, and no one claimed private ownership of any possessions, but everything they owned was held in common. . . . Great grace was upon them all" (vv. 32-33).

While we live in a different type of economy than the early church, my family and I practice generosity in the following ways because we believe that God rewards our faithfulness:

- We pay our tithes, dividing them between the local and national church.

- We give away rather than sell items when we accumulate too much.

- We graciously receive gifts and thank God for the generosity of others.

- We invest in the businesses of our friends. We don't ask for a "hook-up" or free services. We sow into their labor, and we hope people will sow into ours.

- We give additional offerings in times of need.

- We save money for our retirement and rainy days so that we are better positioned to be generous.

GIVING

I encourage pastors to teach on tithing. Ask for donations, and be transparent about how finances are used. I am not necessarily in favor of all the church members voting about finances and the church budget. That just bogs things down and creates unhealthy divisions in the church. Too much of the church finance process can be weaponized. Some voting systems lend themselves to giving power to the biggest donors. Instead of leaders responding to the leading of the Spirit and the needs of the community, they become indebted to Mr. and Mrs. Biggs and their checkbook. I subscribe instead to the principle that God doesn't want us to be overly concerned with how our offering is spent. When we give money to the church, we need to trust that God will direct it where it needs to go. If you don't feel good about that, you need better leaders or a better church.

We should do what we can to ensure that ministries we give to are good stewards of God's money, but we cannot always know for certain that the money we support will be spent correctly or wisely. The church should have a transparent accounting and accountability system in place. Churches should produce annual records and have periodic audits. As a church leader, I know that money can be mismanaged, yet we can't allow ourselves to be overly burdened with this concern, nor should we use this as an excuse not to give. Giving is an act of faith, of generosity, not a vote to coerce or control. Below are a few points that leaders should share about giving.

- Giving is an act of faith recognizing that God is the source of our wealth (James 1:17).

- We should give out of our increase. A tithe (10 percent) is a good starting point. Believers ought to give according to their income (Proverbs 3:9).

- Sowing and reaping is a spiritual law that does work, but it is not some magical quid pro quo. I believe that the law works for both the good and the bad seeds you plant (Galatians 6:7-10).

- God doesn't want money that was given in anger or coerced. The attitude matters as much as the cash. When we give freely to God, we receive freely from God (2 Corinthians 9:7).

A dear friend and I had a debate about money and the accumulation of wealth. I say the accumulation of wealth is relative and that if you are generous, the amount of money you have doesn't matter. My friend says that God cares more about what you keep than what you give away. While I normally agree with him on matters of theology, I disagree with him on this matter of wealth. I believe God cares more about your heart and what you are willing to give than the actual total in your bank account.

A couple of stories come to mind that I think help my argument. First, Jesus did not have a problem with nice or fancy items. When Mary anointed the feet of Jesus with expensive perfume worth a year's wages, he did not complain. Jesus even rebuked Judas Iscariot, saying, "Leave her alone. She bought it" (John 12:7). In other words, the money was hers, and she bought it for a special occasion. You do not have to give every-thing away to others.

The second is the story of the widow's mite in Luke 21, which may seem to discount my argument, but I think the point Jesus is making is that the amount we give is inconse-quential. What matters is that our trust is not in our wealth but in our belief that God will reward and bless us as we give. Our generosity should not be limited by how much we have accu-mulated; it is only limited by our faith. To be generous, you must have the capacity to give. If you have a lot, you can give a lot. If you have little, you can give a little, but the important part is being a cheerful and faithful giver. Ananias and Sapphira were punished in Acts 5 not because of what they kept, but because they lied and reneged on an agreement to be generous. I say, keep what you want but listen to the Spirit of God when the Spirit calls you to be generous.

Interestingly, I think I am the third or fourth owner of the little car I gave away. All the owners have been members of our church. I hope that it continues to bless those in and around our community. If nothing else, I hope that our small act of generosity sparks a fire of paying it forward and inspires the same culture of mutual aid that inspired my wife and me so many years ago.

The church has been a poor steward of the resources we have been given. The bulk of our time is devoted to worship services and insider "fellowship" events that seek only to in-doctrinate the individual into our congregational culture. We create holy huddles rather than facilitating mission and creat-ing capacity that gives hope to the world. Again, we must ask ourselves, What is the mission of the church? Is it to entertain members or to engage the world? Each congregation must ask itself, What is our mission, and is that reflected in our budget plan? Proverbs 3:9-10 says, "Honor the Lord with your substance and with the first fruits of all your produce; then your barns will be filled with plenty, and your vats will be bursting with wine." The proverb not only has meaning for individuals donating to the church, but has meaning for congregations as well. We are tax exempt for a reason. The money we receive as congregations is not to ensure we have comfy seats and premium audiovisuals for our isolated faith community. The funds we receive should honor the Lord and provide a measure of hope to the community.

I love a good worship service. I expect it to have great music, preaching, and visuals. As I mature, though, I realize this Christian walk must be more than entertainment. I have been in church for most of my fifty-plus years. I probably have preached, read, or heard most of the Bible ten times over. I ask, "How can I be a good steward of all the knowledge and wisdom that has been poured into my life?" I urge you, pastors, and leaders, to examine where your resources are going. Are we just maintaining a Sunday fellowship for the elite, or are we equipping people to impact the world? Is it all for a Sunday morning show?

I don't know what your priorities are, but here are some categories that you might consider and see where they are reflected in the work of your ministry:

- Worship for members
- Fellowship and member social events
- Combating issues of poverty
- Social justice and education
- Discipleship
- Community service (childcare and elderly care)
- Prayer and support

Maybe your congregation has other priorities, but I would urge you, as stewards of God's people and money, to wisely examine the management of these precious gifts. Here are a few things we should ask about money in the church:

1. Is there transparency and accountability in your accounting?

2. Who are the true influencers on how church funds are spent?

3. Does the amount of money a person gives affect that person's standing in the congregation?

4. Do you have programs and ministries that, if they were discontinued, would have little negative impact on the church or the community?

5. How much of the church's expenditures reflect "But that's the way we've always done it"?

6. Is the salary paid to staff commensurate with the salary of the population who attends the church services?

7. Is there waste or fraudulent spending?

8. Is debt hindering your church from doing effective ministry?

9. What are the potential unintended consequences of making significant changes in the budget and expenditures?

10. Do you know how church funds given to support missions are being used?

11. Does your church spend too much or too little on physical facilities?

12. Does the church's budget reflect faith, futility, or foolishness?

As we reflect on these questions, we need to understand that budgets are not just business documents—they are moral documents as well. How we use our money matters. Today, many groups are calling for the divestment from this or that enterprise. Issues of human rights, social justice, creation care, and other reasons are often cited. Ironically, these calls often come from people of privilege who, while protesting parts of the process, still want to partake of the benefits of the finished product.

Instead of divesting, maybe we should organize and invest in people and processes that align with our beliefs. Do we try to bend the ethical will of Big Oil, or would our time and energy be better spent finding alternative sources of energy or even alternative ways to get to work? Are we too comfortable trying to change current institutions rather than creating our own? Do we have the energy to come together for the common good to bring about long-term change, even if it means self-sacrifice? Maybe we go without bread ourselves to bring about the change we hope occurs.

Stewardship is about managing our time, talents, and resources. Instead of organizing to withhold, let's organize to strengthen and support what we value and what we believe. Let us educate our members so that they are empowered, building not only the desire to be generous but the capacity as well.

QUESTIONS FOR REFLECTION

1. Does talking about money in ministry energize you or cause your fear? Why?

2. Do you and your family have a healthy practice of money management?

3. What would generosity look like in your congregation?

4. Name one thing that would change for the better in your leadership and in your congregation if you organized your ministry being intentionally mindful of time, talent, and resources?

5. As a leader, what are the creative opportunities for you to increase your generosity?

TEN

Characteristic Eight:
Strategic Leadership Development

> *You should also look for able [leaders] among all the people, [leaders] who fear God, are trustworthy, and hate dishonest gain; set such [leaders] over them as officers over thousands, hundreds, fifties, and tens. Let them sit as judges for the people at all times; let them bring every important case to you but decide every minor case themselves. So it will be easier for you, and they will bear the burden with you. If you do this, and God so commands you, then you will be able to endure, and all these people will go to their home in peace.*
> —EXODUS 18:21-23

ONE OF MY favorite "old timey" church songs says, "Come go with me, the journey is long; come go with me, the journey is long." As leaders, we must lead for the long haul. Good leaders understand that we are called to guide and prepare those who follow us to an eventual destination. We cannot change the past, and the present is simply a matter of circumstance. No leader can fix the current circumstances or erase the pains of the past, but a competent leader can lay the foundation that will help others overcome their past, endure their current situation, and receive the hope of a prosperous future. The wise leader assesses the present and leads not toward what is, but toward what will be. They lead as if they have already received the desired outcome.

The activated church looks beyond its current circumstance and prepares for its desired end.

In turn, the activated church has a long-term plan for leadership development that is shaped by the gifts and calling of those in the community. Through mentoring, education, entrepreneurship, and sound management practices, the activated church continues to grow and thrive. In the garden, God told Adam and Eve to be fruitful and multiply. Similarly, the activated church re-creates itself through developing leaders, exponentially increasing and expanding its reach within the community. In such a congregation, new leaders are trained, and there are excellent opportunities for leadership internships and leadership succession. The tools of success are not consolidated in one person or personality type but are dispersed through the congregation. The leadership knows and understands how to use the gifting of others to maximize the effectiveness of the organization. Leadership is a key component of church growth and relevance.

Jethro's leadership advice to Moses is timeless. In Genesis 18, Jethro instructs the overburdened Moses to appoint trustworthy leaders to serve alongside him. Leaders who hoard power and do everything themselves, no matter how competent or anointed, will not last long. Too many Christian leaders either abdicate authority to boards and structures or set themselves up as the sole authority. Neither model is healthy in the Christian context. As members of a spiritual organization, we should not dismiss the fact that God can and does speak through leaders, although some institutional churches may find this a bit troubling. But that does not mean that leaders are the sole source of discernment when it comes to decision-making. As Jethro points out to Moses, part of good leadership is unmasking the leadership gifts of others and placing capable people in roles to succeed. Aligning gifts to ministry needs is a key step in sustainable and relevant ministry.

Wise leaders ensure that the work they do lives beyond themselves. Strong leadership is important, but I believe that strong leaders have a sense of confidence that allows them not only to think about the present or the present needs of the community, but also to lead with a sense of what the community will need in the future. That was the philosophy of my mentor. He always said, "God won't bless you with more than you can handle." I took that to mean that to be effective and to grow your capacity to impact others rightly, you need to prepare for the increased capacity. There is no need to ask God to give you the means to feed the five thousand hungry folks if you can barely feed five hundred. The preparedness and organizational prowess of the disciples, who were prepared to manage a large crowd, gave space for the miracle of multiplication to happen.

Leadership development increases the capacity of ministries to be able to respond to the needs of their members and the community. Early on, as part of my training, I developed a personal leadership philosophy, a vital exercise in leadership development. In his 1955 memoir, President Harry S. Truman said, "A leader is a [person] who has the ability to get other people to do what they don't want to do, and like it." This statement, in a very general sense, summarizes my philosophy of leadership: a leader is a person who can effectively motivate other people to carry out a specific goal or vision. Consistency of leadership is important in ministry. Good leaders ensure that the vision lives beyond them. Habakkuk 2:2 states, "Then the LORD answered me and said: 'Write the vision and make it plain on tablets, that he may run who reads it'" (NKJV). Churches should consider providing resources for both current and future leaders so that they are ready to run with the vision.

As a graduate of the United States Air Force Academy and a former Air Force officer, I learned a lot about leadership, but as Moses and I both found, leading civilians is very different from leading soldiers. In the military, subordinates do not have much choice; the order is given, and based on the rank hierarchy, the order is carried out. In the military, you do not have to have much of a leadership philosophy. The system is the philosophy, and it is designed to work in a certain way. Most of those within the network adhere to the structure that is set forth. In the civilian world, this is not necessarily the case, and I do not think that military-style or authoritarian leadership works best in the church. In the church, you want people to be able to think for themselves and to be responsive not only to a person in leadership but to the leading of the Holy Spirit. A leader in the military must be able to motivate people to risk their life if so ordered. In the civilian world, it can be a challenge just to get a person to show up for work on time.

Senior leaders need to pay attention to the development and nurturing of young leaders. Letting people walk alongside you has phenomenal benefits in creating a pipeline of potentially strong leaders. My first professional leadership role in ministry was as a youth pastor. I supervised only a few paid staff, but I supervised many volunteer staff. This experience was the beginning of my mentorship into leadership. Watching my pastor work with volunteers was especially instrumental in the development of my leadership philosophy. Calling yourself a leader when people are obligated to follow, or when they depend on you for a paycheck, is one thing, but being able to motivate a group who is voluntarily following you is another. My pastor had the uncanny ability to motivate legions of people to give of their time and selves in the building of our ministry. People left high-paying jobs to come work at our church for a lot less money. I took a $20,000 pay cut to work at that church. Members spent hours of their free time working in the ministry and assisting our pastor.

It was amazing to see the number of people devoted to serving my pastor and his wife. This model of leadership is typical in many African American congregations. In some BIPOC and southern traditions, part of the work of the ministry is also serving the senior pastor and the "first lady." Though the practice can and has been abused, I find significant merit in honoring those in leadership roles. That bias comes from my cultural heritage and probably also from my military background—the mentoring style I've chosen as I've developed as a leader has been tempered by my culture and context, which always matter when you lead people.

I would love to say I was a natural-born leader and never made mistakes. But I made a ton of mistakes. Sometimes I cringe at the decisions I made in my twenties and thirties, even at the ways I treated people. But I learned, and I was always willing to acknowledge my errors. Good leaders don't just pop up overnight. Thankfully, good mentors guide us, chastise us, and support us along the journey. They even help us say "I'm sorry."

Through careful observation and a lot of trial and error, I have developed three codices that form my philosophy of leadership:

1. Take care of your people.

2. Lead by example.

3. Prepare another person to take your place.

TAKE CARE OF YOUR PEOPLE

Without people, the leader is nothing. A teacher cannot teach if there are no students; a pastor is just doing personal devotions if there is no congregation. John Maxwell is clear in his book *Developing the Leader within You* when he says, "Leadership is the ability to obtain followers." Leaders need people to follow them, so it only makes sense that a leader takes care of those who make them a leader. When a leader takes care of those who currently follow, it helps them attract others and pushes the leader to a higher level of leadership. True loyalty is developed when followers are appreciated, compensated, and motivated. If leaders do not take care of their people, the people will not take care of the leaders or buy into the larger vision. Soon such a leader will be alone, with no one following but a shadow. In John 21, Jesus warns Simon Peter several times to "feed my sheep" when Jesus inquires about love. In closing, Jesus says, One day, you are going to be old. You are young now and can dress yourself, but one day you are going to have to depend on others. Leaders should never, ever forget that they serve people. There will always be times in your leadership journey that human kindness will pay off when you, as a leader, need some goodwill credit and trust.

LEAD BY EXAMPLE

Even though I am a person who practices peace, I often find myself reflecting on the words of military leaders. As paradoxical as it may seem, both Christian leaders and military leaders ask us to give our lives for the cause. Plus, I spent ten years in some form of military service, and that training doesn't just evaporate. While the motivation and the reward may be distinct, the rallying cry is often the same. When addressing a group of Virginia Regiment Officers, George Washington said, "Remember that it is the actions, and not the commission, that make the officer, and that there is more expected from him, than the title." Just like in the military, there is often a frocking that takes place. Even in the most contemporary of religious settings a "ranking" occurs, but it is not the title or position that should inspire. It is our lives, our actions, and our faith witness that should give us our distinction as leaders. I believe in leading in the way that I want to be followed. I believe that a leader must be the first partaker. Leaders cannot ask others to do what they are not willing to do. A leader must set the example for the subordinates to follow. This is especially important in the realm of spiritual leadership because of the great cost. Jesus warned his would-be followers about the cost of leadership. "Another said, 'I will follow you, Lord; but let me first say farewell to those at my home.' Jesus said to him, 'No one who puts a hand to the plow and looks back is fit for the kingdom of God'" (Luke 9:61-62). Leading by example helps those in training endure and be prepared for challenges ahead.

I am opposed to neutral leadership. Hire a manager or a robot if you want to claim neutrality. Neutrality in leadership is a destructive force that often allows systematic abuse to continue unchecked. Go back and read the chapter on identity. When you and your leadership team are walking the streets of Anywhere, USA, talking to folks like Pat from Pasadena, do you think they want to be connected to leaders and churches that are neutral when it comes to addressing the evils and oppression in the local community? In the words of my sister, Kimberly "Sweet Brown" Wilkins, "ain't nobody got time for that." If you want to deactivate your church, stand behind neutrality. Justice-minded leadership seeks to have informed, interculturally competent opinions. Sometimes that means standing up against what is and advocating for what should be. Leadership is leading, not taking polls. That is what politicians do.

As a sidenote and a word of caution, neutral leadership structures can also manifest themselves when no one is in charge, or when everyone is in charge. Flat organizations work well in the absence of conflict, but when there is disruption, abuse, or extreme polarization, there is no one capable of breaking the gridlock. Neutral systems don't allow for visionary leadership or clearly defined lines of authority. When everyone is in charge, no one is in charge.

And one more sidenote—the last one, I promise. Someone is always in charge. There may not be official leadership, but there are always influencers in organizations. Again, this is why I think neutral leadership is so problematic. Abuse can occur in any leadership model, but it is more insidious when power is hidden.

PREPARE ANOTHER TO TAKE YOUR PLACE

The final part of my leadership philosophy simply acknowledges the fact that a leader must have a vision to pass on and someone to carry out that vision. I truly believe the vision of the leader should be greater than the personhood of the leader. Leaders should not be so caught up in the here and now that they do not prepare for the future. When a leader dies or retires or moves on, someone should be waiting to take their place. If the leader has not prepared someone to do so, that person was not a very effective leader. A true leader prepares for the future and has a vision that must continue. A true leader will train others to keep that vision alive when the leader is no longer able to do so.

Leaders are not threatened by rising stars. They encourage them. I truly think it is selfish and unethical for leaders to stay in positions longer than their relevance. If you want to lead until you retire, you must keep educating yourself and surrounding yourself with people better than you. Have people who will push you to stay sharp while you share with them the wisdom that comes with longevity. I love learning from younger leaders and telling stories about the good old days. I am not sure if they appreciate hearing the stories as much as I love telling them, but they are gracious enough to indulge me. Why? Because I make space for their ideas and opinions. I give them space to both succeed and fail. Sometimes the preparation process means letting young leaders make the wrong decision (within limits). The good part is that they learn by doing, and you get to share another story as the wise sage. No matter what age you are, your experiences might put you in the category of the wise sage.

As you think about transformational Christian leadership, the twenty-first-century church needs the following sorts of leaders:

• *Leaders who believe in and practice the power of prayer.* Following the example of Christ must be at the heart of church leadership. We can't assume that everyone who wants to be a leader in our churches is someone with the spirit of Christ. An MDiv or other degree measures academic proficiency, not the proficiency of the heart. We need to examine our leaders and pay attention to why they serve and their journey of faith. Church leaders should have a measure of faith and belief in what God can do. They should have leadership goals beyond what we see in the physical realm. It goes beyond some of the systems that I've outlined in this book. Sometimes leadership just comes down to faith. Faith, combined with wisdom, can never be underestimated. "But without faith it is impossible to please [God], for he who comes to God must believe that [God] is, and that [God] is a rewarder of those who diligently seek Him" (Hebrews 11:6 NKJV).

• *Culturally competent leaders.* Our world is changing, and the transformational Christian leader must resist the temptation to fall into the trap of the polarizations that divide our society. The church must be a unifying factor in our community. The gospel is for everyone. The great commission says, "Therefore go and make disciples of all nations, baptizing them in the name of the Father and of the Son and of the Holy Spirit, and teaching them to obey everything I have commanded you. And surely I am with you always, to the very end of the age" (Matthew 28:19-20 NIV). To reach the nations, we must be able to communicate cross-culturally. We must meet people where they are. We must reject Westernized colonialism in our approach to sharing the gospel.

• *Entrepreneurial leaders.* Here are several characteristics of successful entrepreneurs:

  ○ *Creative.* Entrepreneurs are not satisfied with the status quo. They are not interested in why something will not work; they ask, "What will it take to make this happen?"

  ○ *Passionate.* Entrepreneurs are driven and self-motivated. People often tell them to slow down; no one needs to light their fire. It is already burning.

  ○ *Optimistic.* Entrepreneurs never dwell on the past or the negative. Entrepreneurs don't get weighed down by the past. They are perpetually looking forward. They don't focus on the problem in a negative situation. They look for opportunities.

  ○ *Visionary.* Having a strong vision helps propel you toward accomplishment and gives others a path to follow. If there is no vision or apparent purpose, it is challenging to orient and guide a team. Entrepreneurial leaders motivate people because they have a clear, easy-to-articulate vision.

  ○ *Charismatic.* Entrepreneurs connect with people. They never lose sight of the fact that they are ultimately in the business of people. Entrepreneurs know how to gain buy-in from those around them on their big ideas.

○ *Adaptable.* Entrepreneurial leaders understand they must improvise for, adapt to, and overcome the changes that are part of life and the growth process. Anything alive shows signs of growth. The leader who lives a life of purpose continues to stay relevant and continues to grow. As living beings, we must continually reproduce ourselves through our work, and through those we mentor. We must also continuously deal with the ever-shifting circumstances of life. We must adapt. Entrepreneurs know how to adapt to unfamiliar situations. Adaptation can mean learning new skills, changing strategies, or just pushing pause. Whatever it takes, entrepreneurs can improvise, adapt, and overcome, but they approach situations with an open mind and a willingness to change direction if necessary.

○ *Resourceful.* Entrepreneurs also know how to make the most of what they have. They maximize their time, money, and talent at hand. Great leaders calculate every move carefully, and there is always a plan and a purpose to their decision-making process.

○ *Team oriented.* The most successful entrepreneurs have an approach to teamwork like that of a quarterback or a team captain. They are not dissimilar to other types of influential leaders like volleyball team captains or NASCAR pit crew chiefs who rely on the team to accomplish goals. A good quarterback in football, more than in any other sport, is dependent on the team of players around them. "Hero ball" doesn't win championships. Great quarterbacks know how to improvise and adapt, but they are also coachable. They know how to get everyone involved, and they play to the strengths of everyone on the team. A good quarterback knows to get rid of the ball quickly and keep moving forward. Transformational twenty-first-century leaders are not ones to hold all the power, or to isolate themselves. Like the NASCAR crew chief, they understand they must communicate and help everyone integrate into the work of the ministry, even if they don't get the glory of driving the car. The captain on a volleyball team can't play all the positions, but the captain can put people in the position to win. A good volleyball team captain has excellent administration skills, thorough knowledge of the game, respect for other team members, dedication, and the ability to motivate and inspire team members even in adversity.

Of all the leadership lessons I have learned, the ones from my mother stand out the most. As I look back at why I serve, and why I am a leader in the church, I realize that my true leadership journey started when at five or six years old I began making the Kool-Aid for my mother's Sunday school class. She was my first Sunday school teacher, and she taught me the importance of serving in God's kingdom. Shoestring potato chips and Kool-Aid were the snacks that we took to church each Sunday. I remember the brown plastic pitcher that I had to hold each Sunday as we drove to Pine Crest Presbyterian Church in Houston's historic Fifth Ward. It was my job not only to make the Kool-Aid but to keep it safe from spilling (a job that I wasn't always successful at).

Mixing sugary beverages may not seem as profound a spiritual lesson as what is suggested in Deuteronomy 6—"recite [these words] to your children and talk about them when you are at home and when you are away"—but it was how my mother taught me the gospel message of service. No matter what, my mother taught me that if God gave you a gift, you needed to use it to serve God's people. Whether it was singing in the choir or baking cookies for fellowship hour, my mother and I were involved in it. She set an example of service that I could not ignore. When youth ministry opportunities or trips came up, she made sure I could attend, even when money was tight. Sometimes I went to camps and meetings alone, taking the Trailways bus line on my own. At times I was the only child at an adult leadership conference. I learned so much, and the church became such a fun part of my childhood experience that something deep inside of me said, "No matter what you do in life, part of the time you spend living should be spent sharing the good news of Christ." That voice speaks to me often. Even when I want to quit, it speaks to me. My mother was by no means a perfect parent, but I am glad she introduced me to a perfect Savior.

IN IT FOR THE LONG HAUL

Churches that are engaged in leadership development allow people to use their gifts, no matter how small. Leadership development in the church doesn't start at the age of eighteen, or when students go to seminary—it can start in the kindergarten class with a little kid making Kool-Aid, straightening hymnals, or lighting candles for worship. Strategic leadership development is helping people see and utilize their God-given gifts. The leader who must do everything and make every decision is not a good leader. Those leaders burn out, and the ministry is consumed along with them. For leadership development to be successful, it must be a long-term practice and priority. You also must recognize that every person you mentor or spend time with is not going to become a leader. There is a lot of heartbreak and disappointment when it comes to strategic leadership development. That does not mean that it is not worth it. Even Jesus was betrayed by one of his twelve trusted disciples. Every frog you kiss is not going to turn into a prince, and how many princes can you hold on to anyway?

Imagine that you lead a ministry of fifty people, but the church has set its goal to double within the next three years. Leading for the long haul means that you are prepared for this growth. You have envisioned how all fifty of your new congregants will fit into your building. You have updated your systems and procedures so that you can effectively minister to and track the new families and individuals who will soon grace your doors. You ignore those who say, "Give me that old-time religion." I say, honor the past by charting a new path. Chart the path to a bright future, a future that honors the contributions of those who came before, yet is not held hostage by their ghosts.

As the apostle Paul was headed to Rome, he understood that the path to his destination would be fraught with danger (Acts 27–28). He tried to warn those with him about the perils they would soon face. When the tempestuous Mediterranean northeast wind, the Euroclydon (my favorite word in the Bible), arose, Paul was ready. Paul's ability to follow the voice of God amid the storm and lead for the long haul allowed 276 persons to have the hope of a prosperous future. Amid leading others, Paul was bitten by a venomous viper, which he quickly shook off into the fire. Many of the native people who witnessed this expected Paul to die, since that is what history dictated. What they did not understand was that God had a purpose for Paul that gave him power that far exceeded the current expectations of humankind. Paul was leading for the long haul, and nothing was going to deter him from reaching his God-ordained destination, not even a viper, not even the Euroclydon's violent agitation.

Here are three things (which I think sound much better in Spanish) that long-haul leaders should keep in mind:

- *Muévete (move it)*. Move toward your vision of the future. Don't just stand around navel-gazing and stagnant in the present, but move forward in faith and with sound practices. You don't get from point A to point B by sitting still.

- *Sacúdete (shake it)*. As you lead for the long haul, you might experience a few bumps and bruises along the way.

You may feel that you are in the middle of a violent storm or stranded on a desert island with unfamiliar faces. You might even get bitten once or twice, but you can't wallow in self-pity or get depressed and die. As a God-ordained leader, you must shake it off.

- *Soportate (endure it).* Put in place policies, procedures, and systems that will enhance the vision for the long haul.

Long-haul plans need support. A long-haul trucker driving from Kalona, Iowa, to Los Angeles, California, will make sure that the truck is in tip-top shape. The truck will be filled with fuel, the route will be mapped, and the tire pressure will be just right. The trucker will be well-rested and understand the length of the journey ahead. Why? So both the driver and cargo arrive at the destination safely and on time.

Once we begin leading for the long haul, we can settle into roles and our work and carry out our mission with confidence, "preaching the kingdom of God and teaching the things which concern the Lord Jesus Christ" (Acts 28:31 NKJV), in whatever capacity the Lord has called us.

QUESTIONS FOR REFLECTION

1. Who is responsible for developing leaders in your church?

2. How will you train and vet leaders?

3. What are the opportunities to serve in your church and your programs?

4. Where are the places that children and youth can plug in?

5. How easy is it for people to get involved in your congregation?

6. How are you ensuring the safety and well-being of people you are mentoring?

Conclusion

The spirit of the Lord GOD is upon me,
because the LORD has anointed me;
he has sent me to bring good news to the oppressed,
to bind up the brokenhearted,
to proclaim liberty to the captives,
and release to the prisoners;
to proclaim the year of the LORD's favor,
and the day of vengeance of our God;
to comfort all who mourn.
—ISAIAH 61:1-2

RIGHT BEFORE HE is clubbed in the head, the dying man in the Monty Python sketch says, "I think I'll go for a walk." But it is too late—onto the refuse pile he goes. But it is not too late for us church leaders. The church is not dead yet. I know that the church is very much alive. I see it in the eyes of so many young men and women whom I come in contact with each day. There is still a chance to change our trajectory of decline. Think about what resulted from one interaction between Philip and the Ethiopian in the early church. It brought together many different cultures. Their encounter highlights what can happen when the church engages those outside our own culture. If you are reading this book, you have the knowledge, the desire, and an understanding of the holy power available to you to be a bridge builder, helping facilitate transformation. The right leader and the right team are the sparks we need to activate our church toward relevance. We have to facilitate the transformation that is most needed for the people and communities we serve.

It is time for the church to let go of the old and to reignite the passion that helped bring transformation to the world. It is time for the church to put our faith in God's Spirit, as well to begin to practice sound leadership principles so that we can be activated for ministry in the twenty-first century. If you want to consider yourself an activated church leader, never forget that our congregations and ministry programs should exist to serve the body or to equip the body. If we are struggling to keep the doors open and our only purpose is to raise more funds or get more members, is that the future we want? Who wants their entire existence to be getting up, going to work to make money, coming home, and pressing repeat? I sure don't. I want my life to mean something. I don't just want to exist for the sake of existing or to live my life solely to produce widgets, without getting the opportunity to live life. I want to live a life of purpose, where I am answering God's call. I want to give hope to others and to share with them the transformative power of God's love. We should want more for ourselves, and from the institutions to which we are connected.

As you read this book, I hope you gleaned some ideas about how the activated church should look. I hope you are motivated to move beyond cultural traditions and to birth new life into your local church. Hyun Hur, cofounder and director of ReconciliAsian in Pasadena, California, talking to a group of pastors concerning moving our church denomination forward, said, "I feel we have lost our vision, and it needs to be reignited. I came to this church to be part of a different narrative—a countercultural, anti-Christendom movement that follows a radical Jesus. We need to go back to the beginning—our radical reformation theology—and reignite the vision in our own context." As I wrote earlier, the church needs to create a culture of people who buy into the vision. We have to know our identity, and we have to demonstrate or live into that identity as we serve the community. Strong, culturally competent leadership will guide the activated church to effortless victory in accomplishing its mission, not because of a cult of personality, but because the mission and the leadership are grounded in and connected to the movement of God's Spirit. A clearly defined vision and the clarity it brings will set the active church apart, creating motion. That motion will drive the mission and the people, reducing distractions and needless division.

If we want to become an activated church, we must pay attention to those on the margins, not just those in the power centers of our community. Some of our institutional factions are taking desperate measures to hold on to their power, like a body seizing in the last throes of death (to return to the image from the Monty Python sketch). Others have decided to become neutral and are slowly fading into the background or springing up like a bitter political cult cutting itself off from the rest of the church body. But there are a few leaders who still believe that there is hope for the future of our Christian churches. There is a new generation on the horizon that I know will have the ability to bridge the gap. They will once again help others realize that the church is a place of refuge and transformation. We know that we cannot do it alone. The activated church depends on the people inside and outside the church. It serves, it connects with, and it feeds those entrusted to its care, from leaders to members to the people on the street.

I pray we can be the church that God has called us to be. Now, go, be the church.

QUESTIONS FOR REFLECTION

1. How is your ministry bringing about transformation to the community you serve?

2. What is your biggest distraction as a church leader that limits your ability to help bring transformation to the people in your community?

3. What is the best piece of advice you can share for church leaders who want to have an impact on their community?

4. What are the cultural blinders that keep you from seeing God at work in your community?

5. What are the administrative systems you have in place that are no longer working?

6. Do you still have a passion for engaging your community?

Resources

Identity Factors That May Affect Your Diversity
and Inclusion Efforts

A Guide for Intentional Diversity in
Congregations

Event or Community Program Checklist

Responding to Crisis as a Congregation

Concert of Prayer Sample Format

Profile of Leaders Interviewed for This Book

Identity Factors That May Affect Your Diversity and Inclusion Efforts

The activated church, depending on your location, may deal with the following identity factors for people who wish to be a part of your congregation.

1. **Religion/spirituality.** Religious identity is what ultimately draws the church together and should be the common bond of any congregation. Religion can be a central part of one's identity. The word *religion* comes from a Latin word that means "to tie or bind together." We base our religious identity on our shared beliefs and rituals, centering on the spiritual part of being. We must agree that this is the unwavering aspect of community and identity and not compromise. The culture of our fellowship should be evident. People need to understand who we are, why we do what we do, and where we hope to land as we progress as disciples of Christ. I believe churches must always be clear about this aspect of their identity and should encourage people who are not comfortable with that proclaimed identity to find a more suitable place to worship. Does this mean that everyone who receives services or partners with the church must share exactly the same religious beliefs or identity? Absolutely not (see chapter 6 for more detail). But the core of the church must understand the mission of the church and agree with that mission or understand how change and vision-casting happens.

2. **Race.** Race is a manufactured or socially constructed set of criteria used to distinguish a group of people based on physical characteristics. Racial identity in the United States is based primarily on skin color, black and white. Racial identity as a social construct is also interwoven with ethnicity.

3. **Ethnicity.** Ethnic identity refers to a person's social identity within a broader context based on membership in a cultural or social group. Ethnicity takes into consideration religion, language, customs, nationality, and other cultural factors. Because language,

nationality, and religious upbringing are part of ethnic identity, ethnicity can have a significant impact on how congregations relate to and reach their members in the community. There can be language barriers, differing understandings of gender roles, and other cultural taboos that need addressing when serving people of different ethnic backgrounds.

4. **Sexual orientation.** Sexual orientation "describes a person's enduring physical, romantic, or emotional attraction to another person. Gender identity and sexual orientation are not the same. Transgender people may be straight, lesbian, gay, bisexual, or queer. For example, a person who transitions from male to female and is attracted solely to men would typically identify as a straight woman."[1] The topic of LGBTQIA+ inclusion has been a challenging problem for church leaders and especially for LGBTQIA+ people who feel a call to serve and be a part of their local congregation. As a denominational leader, I have had to lead people with varying opinions on the inclusion of people who identify as LGBTQIA+. I sincerely believe that God calls us to bring healing and hope to everyone in our communities. Christ himself did not fail to engage with the outcasts or people on the fringes. The lines we draw as mere mortals are not the same lines God has called us to honor. Jesus interacted with everyone from tax collectors to Samaritans to winebibbers. They were people whom some in the faith community of Jesus' times deemed unclean, but Jesus still felt compelled to serve.

5. **Gender identity and expression.** The traditional views of gender are changing in our society. There are contrasting views about which the church needs to be mindful. One view has been that gender identity resides within the individual. However, others challenge this assumption by arguing that gender identity is created in the context of interactions, societal structures, and cultural expectations[2] and that gender identity is "a person's internal, deeply held sense of their gender." Gender expression is the "external manifestations of gender, expressed through a person's name, pronouns, clothing, haircut, behavior, voice, and/or body

characteristics. Society identifies these cues as masculine and feminine."[3] Gender identity involves more than the anatomical—it involves the inner knowledge and outer expression of one's gender.

6. **Abilities.** Ability identity refers to possessing a positive sense of self and feelings of connection to, or solidarity with, the disability community. U.S. churches need to think about what this means beyond being compliant with the Americans with Disabilities Act (ADA) or having their building up to code. Understanding ability identity also means helping individuals adapt to a disability, including navigating related social stresses and daily hassles. When relating to people who have physical and other disabilities, a congregation should create plans that contain relevant content and goals linked to specific disabilities. According to the American Psychological Association, "Disability identity should guide people with disabilities toward what to do, what to value and how to behave in those situations where their disability stands out, as well as those where it is not salient."[4] The organization lists six disability narratives that highlight issues of disability identity:

- *Communal attachment.* People with disabilities are actively engaging with their peers thanks to shared experiences.

- *Affirmation of disability.* Personal affirmation of disability is a way to feel included in society by having the same rights and responsibilities as others and by being recognized and treated equally.

- *Self-worth.* Self-worth is valuing oneself and one's skills.

- *Pride.* Being proud of one's identity and, in the process, acknowledging possessing a socially devalued quality, such as a mental or physical disability. Pride encourages people with disabilities to own rather than hide their disability.

- *Discrimination.* This narrative speaks to the awareness that people with disabilities are often the recipients of bias and prejudice within their daily life.

- *Personal meaning and disability.* Searching for significance and finding benefits associated with a disability is an essential aspect of disability identity because it can represent acceptance.

7. **Nationality.** Nationality is generally a political term describing "a people having a common origin, tradition, and language, and capable of forming or constituting a nation-state."[5] Many first-generation church groups are formed around nationality, often because of language barriers, political concerns, and other traditions.

8. **Socioeconomic status.** The social standing or class of an individual or group. This is another area where congregations tend to be homogenous when you look at education, income, and occupation. While many churches serve the poor or reach out to the underprivileged, those same connections don't exist within the membership of the congregation. Examinations of socioeconomic status often reveal inequities in access to resources, plus issues related to privilege, power, and access.

9. **Generational.** Age or generational diversity is one of the many identity factors that we need to pay attention to, especially if other identity factors are more homogenous. Currently, five generations will primarily affect our ministries. Millennials are now the largest generation, and many of them are fast approaching middle age. Information sources will vary slightly on the beginning and ending date of each generation, so I have included the data that is most commonly used. I have also included the percentage of the population that each age cohort represented in 2019.

- Generation Z, or Zoomers: Born 1997–TBD (23 percent)

- Millennials, or Generation Y: Born 1981–1996 (24 percent)

- Generation X: Born 1965–1980 (22 percent)

- Baby boomers: Born 1946–1964 (23 percent)

- Traditionalists, or silent generation: Born in or before 1945 (7 percent)

Each generation has significantly different understandings of institutional authority, leadership, institutional stability, technology, and communication. The activated church must understand this as it seeks to connect with the broader community. We are experiencing seismic shifts in organizational culture, mainly because we're shifting from baby boomer leadership to Generation X leadership. While loyal to the institution, Gen Xers are radical and independent enough to challenge the status quo. Here is a word of warning to churches looking at reaching the next generation: You can't run your church in the same way you have been running it for the past twenty years. If you are gearing up for millennials, be careful, Generation Z are the new kids on the block. Many of the negative attitudes we have toward millenials might be more connected to the normal generation gap that occurs between groups. Millennials are in their mid-twenties to early forties. Older Gen Zers are exiting college and will soon fill up the workforce en masse and will be returning home to the community. They are the children of Gen Xers, so they are likely to be responsive to the leadership style of Generation X, which is quite different from the now elder millennials. Don't gear up for millenials, gear up for a multigeneration congregation that is intentional about nurturing and including members throughout life's journey.

A Guide for Intentional Diversity in Congregations

This guide exists as an intentional effort to make space for all people to exercise power, voice, and worship. For this to happen, we must transform the way we plan our gatherings, how we lead, and our assumptions as we reach out to the community.

This guide is not prescriptive. It is just that, a guide to help you determine what type of intentional diversity and inclusion you wish to pursue. We can't be all things to all people. And some of us are not equipped to handle all forms of diversity. There are limitations based on our theology, our beliefs, and even our exposure. We also must face the reality of the communities to which we belong, understanding that diversity is just simply variety. That variety differs based on our geographical location.

The church leadership reflects the constituency

- Who is on the church leadership team? What do they look like demographically?

- Does the leadership of the congregation represent the groups who will be invited to worship?

- Who is not invited to be in leadership? Why is that? Has the decision to exclude been made based on Scripture, theology, tradition, or for other reasons?

- What assumptions about leadership does the dominant culture have?

- What orientation is provided for (new) members and newly appointed leaders? Is someone assigned as a mentor for new members or attendees to help them become familiarized with the culture?

- Do we have space for caucusing (for women/men, different age groups, various ethnic groups, sexual orientations, and other natural identity factors)?

Space is created to empower all to exercise their power/participation

- Can members speak into the work of the congregation?

- Who is creating the agenda? Who is facilitating meetings?

- How many ideas come from the dominant culture? What voices carry the most weight?

- Do we understand the difference between the tokenization of voices and the empowerment of voices?

- If there are congregational business meetings and voting, where and when do the meetings take place? For whom is it convenient?

- Are childcare and transportation available? How are we considering the difficulty of volunteering for single parents or those with other types of responsibilities and job schedules?

Event/project goals speak to the concerns of the constituency (underrepresented groups)

- How do the concerns and issues of people of color shape the agenda of the congregation?

- Where are the entry points into the conversation between the dominant culture and non-dominant groups related to worship services or other ministry projects?

- What agenda or cultural practices might the dominant culture need to give up?

- Do the themes, examples, and images used for a gathering represent a dominant/disempowering narrative?

Communication styles reflect the constituency

- *Planning:* What are the planning group members' preferences related to communication? Do people respond to email, letters, phone calls, social media? What assumptions do group members carry about effective communication? (Do we expect to receive RSVPs, or do we trust that people will come if they know about a meeting or event?)

- *Practice:* Who is in front of the audience, leading and speaking? What tone is set by the opening gathering for the entire event?

- Who is serving in the background?

The work project/event reflects equality and respect among diverse people and groups, not a victim/hero/villain relationship

- How is mutuality fostered in relationship-building across differences?

- How are we talking about race (or sexuality or gender)? Are we framing diversity as an obstacle to be dealt with or a gift to be celebrated?

- Who is talking and who is listening?

- Is there an identity-driven divide between who is "being helped" and who is "helping"?

- Do the event's themes represent a dominant/disempowering narrative or a shared narrative of becoming inclusive communities?

White people work on educating themselves on internalized superiority, and people of color work on educating themselves on internalized inferiority

(You can insert *cisgender superiority* or *generational superiority* here as well.)

- *Planning:* How does internalized superiority maintain white power and privilege in our context? (Are we expecting people of color to educate the dominant culture on issues of race?) How will we address this?

- *Practice:* Are we providing space during our planning to discuss how internalized superiority or internalized inferiority might be at play? Are we providing an antiracist framework for a multicultural experience? Are we debriefing afterward? Who is responsible for debriefing?

Event or Community Program Checklist

If we are going to partner with other organizations or open our events to the community, we need to ensure that we consider who will show up and how we can be welcoming to new people who may not be used to our traditions or values. Use this checklist to evaluate your planning process and possible event venues to ensure that they are inclusive and welcoming for all participants. While you will likely be unable to answer all of these questions in the affirmative for all venues, by confirming this information and sharing it with attendees, you can help ensure that attendees can make informed decisions about your event. Event planners or organizers can make the appropriate accommodations or contingency plans. You will also be prepared to answer questions.

Planning process

- The planning committee is inclusive and represents the diversity of our constituency.

- We have a written code of conduct for participants.

- We have budgeted for inclusiveness. (It is crucial to include accommodation costs in your planning. Your initial budget should allow for the potential charges for providing accommodation services you might need.)

Inclusive spaces

- Is the entrance accessible for those with mobility issues?

  o Are doorways sufficiently wide (32 inches from one side of of the doorframe to the opposite side)?

  o Are doorways automatic?

  o Is there step-free access?

  o If there is a wheelchair lift, is there an alternative for those who cannot do stairs but do not use a wheelchair?

  o Is there disability access parking?

  o Is there a space to be dropped off in front of the accessible entrance or nearby?

- Is the event location on an accessible floor? (Note: Some event spaces are on the upper floors. Do not assume that the space you have reserved is on the ground floor without confirmation.)

- Does the event have a clear policy allowing service animals? The law requires access, but it is good to confirm this so that there won't be any confusion.

  o Are event staff adequately trained in the policy permitting service animals?

- ○ Does the venue have relief areas for service animals?

- Does the event permit emotional support animals?

- How are the acoustics for conversations? Will it be difficult for hard-of-hearing attendees to participate?

- Is there sufficient lighting?

- Does the venue use strobe or other flashing lights? (These may cause seizures for some participants.)

- What is the layout of the room? Are aisles thirty-six inches wide and free of barriers? Is there accessible, integrated seating available throughout the space?

- Is there an accessible restroom?

  - ○ Is the accessible restroom on the same floor as the event or reachable by the elevator?

  - ○ With sufficiently wide doorways?

  - ○ With an automatic doorway?

  - ○ With step-free access?

  - ○ With sufficiently large stalls or dedicated single-occupant restrooms?

- Is there adequate marked signage? (For example, braille and tactile language or easy-to-read fonts and large font size.)

  - ○ Restrooms?

  - ○ Entrances and exits?

  - ○ Elevators?

  - ○ Drop-off and pick-up points?

Cost

- What is the overall cost of food and drink? (This can be a range or approximate.)

- Are there adequate options that are less expensive?

Beverages

Beverages are tricky for religious events and programs. It all depends on the type of event you are having. Is it a community or interfaith event?

- Are non-alcoholic beverages available?

- Are sugar-free beverages available?

- Are kosher beverages available?

- Are halal beverages available?

Food

- Is vegetarian food available?

- Is vegan food available?

- Is gluten-free food available?

- Is kosher food available?

- Is halal food available?

- Can the restaurant or location accommodate food allergies? If so, does it require advance notice?

- Does the event carry epinephrine pens, and is the staff adequately trained in recognizing and immediately addressing allergic reactions?

- Does the restaurant or location provide large-print or braille menus?

- Is there a children's menu available?

Miscellaneous

- What is the overall noisiness of the venue (scale of one to five)?

- Is there a private lactation room? Are nursing parents welcome to nurse in public?

- Is there a separate quiet space for those who need to step away?

If planning an additional offsite event, consider these questions:

- Does the venue have a theme (influencing the architecture, staff, food, music, or overall presentation of the venue)? Is the venue's theme respectful and appropriate for a community event?

- For what style of event is this venue best suited? For example, is it a place for a sit-down dinner or for standing conversation?

- Is the location accessible by public transportation? How will attendees travel to the venue? For events held at a hotel, hotel staff usually can recommend companies that provide accessible vans for transportation. If you are planning a social event during a conference, you may want to contact the conference manager for information on any available resources.

- Does the venue have a specific dress code? If so, what is it?

LGBTQIA+ friendliness

Get the language right to be more inclusive. Practice using gender-neutral language and appropriate pronouns. It is also important to avoid hurtful or outdated terms.

Unlike its precedents, modern English no longer considers gender an inflectional category. The only traces of the Old English gender system are gendered pronouns. There are, however, gendered nouns such as *waiter* and *waitress*, *mailman*, and so on. Many nonbinary and genderqueer people prefer gender-neutral nouns to be used to describe them.

- Is the establishment advertised as LGBTQIA+ friendly? (In addition to reading through the venue website, check Yelp, social media, and other reviews.)

- Is an all-gender restroom available?

- What are the restroom policies?

- Can people state pronouns on their nametags or other identification documents?

Multigenerational events

Know who is coming to the event and what they value.

Reaching various generations means understanding their values, life experiences, and formational factors. Each generation makes decisions in different ways. Remember, most of us are serving five generations. We must learn how to adjust to a multigenerational workforce.[6]

Traditionalists

Shaped by: The Great Depression, World War II, radio and movies

Motivated by: Respect, recognition, providing long-term value to the organization

Communication style: Personal touch, handwritten notes instead of email

Worldview: Obedience over individualism; age equals seniority; advancing through the hierarchy

Event considerations: Aging population with physical challenges. They are financially stable but on fixed incomes. They may have more free time to attend events. Provide volunteer opportunities to allow them to contribute to the event.

Baby boomers

Shaped by: The Vietnam War, the civil rights movement, Watergate

Motivated by: Institutional loyalty, teamwork, duty

Communication style: Whatever is most efficient, including phone calls and face-to-face; still have a connection to printed materials

Worldview: Achievement comes after paying one's dues; sacrifice for success

Event considerations: Clearly defined themes, details, and precise schedules. Provide written evaluation forms and offer coaching-style seminar experiences. They are leaving the workforce. This group has been in their peak earning years. They may also be leading boards and supervising decision-makers; millennials may challenge them, but they are also the parents of millennials.

Generation X

Shaped by: The AIDS epidemic, the fall of the Berlin Wall, the dot-com boom, MTV

Motivated by: Diversity, work-life balance, their personal-professional interests rather than the company's or institution's interests

Communication style: Whatever is most efficient, including phone calls and face-to-face; they are digital immigrants

Worldview: Favoring diversity; quick to move on if their employer fails to meet their needs; resistant to change at work if it affects their personal lives

Event considerations: Give them immediate feedback; provide flexible schedules and build-your-own experiences; extend opportunities for personal development; they are independent and entrepreneurial-minded; they are becoming empty-nesters who are looking for new adventures

Millennials

Shaped by: Columbine, 9/11, the Internet

Motivated by: Responsibility, the quality of their manager, unique work experiences

Communication style: IMs, texts, social media, and email. Millennials have grown up with smartphones and tablets.

Worldview: Seeking challenge, growth, and development; fun work life and work-life balance; unlike baby boomers, past understandings of institutional loyalty do not apply; they are more likely to switch from organization to organization as they explore factors that are important to them

Event considerations: Flexible on their schedule; tools to provide immediate feedback; use apps and tech; provide options; plan activities and themes with a purpose; be mindful of carbon footprint related to the event; clean eating options; fitness options; they have young families

Generation Z

Shaped by: Life after 9/11, the Great Recession, access to technology from a young age

Motivated by: Diversity, personalization, individuality, creativity

Communication style: IMs, texts, social media

Worldview: Self-identify as digital device addicts; value independence and individuality; prefer to work with millennial managers, innovative coworkers, and new technologies

Event considerations: Make sure your website is smartphone friendly; make use of the cell phone for engagement; this group may have the least amount of finances, as they are just entering the workforce; offer opportunities for multisensory activities; use Instagram and Snapchat; think Gen X, but younger and more tech-savvy (Gen Xers are their parents); diversity and inclusion should be considered the norm, embrace it.

Know how they learn

We have more ways to acquire knowledge now than ever before, and each generation has become accustomed to these new information streams in very specific ways. You'll find people who expect a lecture-based presentation that combines a knowledgeable speaker with printed materials; these people fall into the traditional generation and baby boomer demographics. Millennials are comfortable acquiring information through e-learning programs, new tech-based experiences (like gaming or virtual reality), and collaborative groups that offer a more active, social environment. Gen Xers bridge the gap. They believe learning should be fun and prefer small group discussions and workshops, but Gen Xers may not find the latest tech offerings, like gaming, to be an effective way to engage at an event.

Rely on the basic human experience

How can you appeal to all these vastly different styles at once? Create an experience that speaks to the fundamentals in all of us. What drives us as humans? What is the basic desire that has brought your audience to your event? After answering these questions, craft a basic message that can be packaged and delivered to your audience in various ways.

Host a seminar with printed materials and memorable visuals for the traditional generation and baby boomers. Bring in experts for a panel Q&A or workshop session for the Gen X crowd and offer them plenty of opportunities to mix with their peers to share ideas. Millennials will want the convenience of having downloadable capabilities for information and an active social media presence with original content they can share through their networks.

Tell an effective story and establish a strong visual identity

A compelling story is key to your event's success, so make sure its message is relatable on a human level that can be adapted to fit each group while still retaining cohesive brand identity. Consider visual messages with infographics, memes, videos, and audio content that is easily shared across the cyberworld. Gen Xers will explore all that is offered and find the material that suits them best.

Meet all groups on their playing field

After you plan your event story/theme, think about how to use the many channels into which your audience taps. Integrate your traditional media with your social media to create a program that contains several options for your audience to connect with, learn from, and pass on through their networks.

While a subsection of the traditional generation and baby boomers groups prefer printed materials, advertising, and direct communication, don't rule out appealing to them through social media as well. Gen Xers are comfortable with social media channels like Facebook, Twitter, or Instagram and turn to blogs for a deeper understanding of the issues.

Millennials and Generation Z are already used to e-learning and are very active on their social networks and across multiple channels.

Know what's relevant and topical

Everyone is looking to your organization to be the expert on your issue, so you must provide relevant, up-to-date information. Connect with your audience with a story.

POST-EVENT

Put a system in place to monitor progress

- How are we evaluating event success?
- What barriers keep certain groups from responding to an evaluation (language, technology, communication modes)?
- Who do we ask to evaluate our work through the lens of the antiracism/anti-oppression continuum?
- Are we bringing in resource people from the outside (for example, those trained in antiracism)?
- What did we learn? How will our next gathering look different thanks to what we learned this time?

- Does the evaluation for participants reflect the importance of mutuality in relationship-building across identity differences?

- What can we celebrate?

Responding to Crisis as a Congregation

Understanding holistic witness means understanding the role of the church before, during, and after a crisis. The outside media world may shift its attention to the next big story, but human needs are always there. While pandemics may be rare, disasters and illness are not. One of the interesting things that occurred during the COVID-19 crisis is that the U.S. government turned to the leaders of industry to help solve problems. Wal-Mart and Target gladly opened their parking lots to serve as triage bases to help curb the spread of COVID-19. In the United States, businesses are considered the champions of society. What would have happened if churches had opened themselves up as willingly as these two retail giants? I am pretty sure there are many more church parking lots than Wal-Marts and Targets. Even though logistically, it was probably easier to contact two CEOs than thousands of pastors, it grieves me to see that for-profit corporations may be better equipped to serve the community than the church.

How can the church better prepare for the future? When disaster strikes, when injustice poisons our community, churches need to have plans in place that allow them to rise to the occasion in disaster relief or community support. The church always has a role to play when our communities are hurting, and pastors and church leaders need to be compassionate and creative as we identify ways to serve our communities and meet their needs. Churches cannot position themselves as takers in the community; we should instead position ourselves as storehouses of good ready to let that good flow out during times of need.

First, churches should identify reliable, local sources of information

Our culture is facing a crisis of trust in its institutions and information sources. In a crisis, church leaders must identify reliable information at the local, state, and national levels to stay updated on recent developments. Likewise, churches can mutually learn from one another about best practices and effective strategies. Depending on the conflict at hand, churches can establish a variety of response teams based on members who are skilled professionals and tradespeople. Churches can partner with experts from other groups. These are the partnerships that are essential. Examples of such groups are Mennonite Disaster Service, Catholic Charities USA, and Presbyterian Disaster Assistance.

While your church may not be able to mobilize nationally, there are opportunities to establish relationships with and support faith-based organizations that can assist your local community in times of need. There are ways that the church can mobilize just as efficiently as Wal-Mart and Target if we are willing to work together.

Second, churches should assess their practices

Even if churches aren't sure what they should change, they can at least begin by better understanding what they are currently doing and what their capacity is in relation to times of need. Churches can evaluate their procedures and seek to enhance them, considering emerging information and guidance. Here are a few areas to consider when developing a crisis response plan:

- A communication plan to reach members

- Communication with community officials and law enforcement. (Do we have the necessary partnerships and contact information?)

- Threat-level plans for various scenarios

   o   Mass shootings

   o   Child abuse (internal and external)

- ° A natural or environmental disaster (specifically for your location)
- ° Extended school closing
- ° Shelter capability of your facility
- ° Online giving capability
- ° Online meeting/service capability
- ° Medical emergencies

Third, churches should overcommunicate their plans

Communicating with members is an essential part of keeping people calm during a time of crisis. It's not enough to simply change what your church is doing. Church leaders must also be intentional about communicating their plans to their people. Tweeting out a prayer is not enough. Quoting Scripture and saying "Trust God," while true, will most likely not be enough to ease fears. It is important to let people know what has changed, why these shifts are taking place, and how the plans will help. Intentional communication can both encourage those who are scared and satisfy those who are skeptical. Churches should have tailored messaging for those most impacted by the crisis. Depending on the situation, it might also be wise to provide information to parents in the congregation about how to have appropriate conversations about the crisis with their children.

Fourth, churches should encourage their people

We should never lose sight of the fact that we are in the people business and that we are people of faith. We need to respond in that manner even as we prepare and plan. The Bible does not tell us to avoid preparation or prayer. Faith without the accompanying works is dead.

> Unless the LORD builds the house,
>   those who build it labor in vain.
> Unless the LORD guards the city,

> the guard keeps watch in vain.
> It is in vain that you rise up early
>   and go late to rest,
> eating the bread of anxious toil;
>   for he gives sleep to his beloved. (Psalm 127:1-2)

When people in your church are either dismayed or dismissive, we can reassure them that God honors both our wise planning and our prayer. While responding to crises such as the global pandemic of 2020, hurricanes, earthquakes, and other disasters may seem overwhelming, the church is uniquely poised to confront the personal challenges of a panicked people with the hope and promises of God's Word. Holistic witness means taking a radical approach to the gospel. Churches and denominations must move beyond the safety of what has always been to see what God is doing in the streets, in the city, in the towns.

Concert of Prayer Sample Format

A concert of prayer is a calling together of God's people to pray. There are times of silent prayer, prayer in small groups, and prayer as an entire gathered group. The concert can be any length of time you need, but I recommend 30 to 60 minutes for your first few. You can go longer as people become more comfortable. There is no limit to the variations of flow and themes, and the mix of prayer formats that can be put into a concert of prayer.

Leaders needed:

- *Group prayer leaders*—I like to spread the true "prayer warriors" or people more comfortable with prayer around to help onstage and in individual groups.

- *Main Scripture reader or emcee*—This person guides the concert, reading Scripture, keeping time, and reminding people of themes.

- *Worship or music leader*—I recommend a choir or band as part of the experience. (Instrumental music can play softly during times of prayer if this fits your tradition).

Order of service for concert of prayer

Opening

Reading of opening theme Scripture

Opening hymn or song of praise: After the song, the leader instructs participants to give short prayers of praise and thanks offered spontaneously from the group.

Statement of purpose: Brief teaching on the importance of communal prayer.

Centering Prayer—People break into groups of 4 or 5 people

Thematic Prayer Sections

The ACTS model (Adoration, Confession, Thanksgiving, Supplication) is an easy way to start, but you can insert themes that fit the needs and focus of your groups. I would limit the prayer sections to four or five to ensure the time is targeted to the theme of the service).

Section 1: Adoration prayers (or other themes appropriate for your group focus)[1]

- ○ Emcee gives short introduction/prayer (depending on your faith tradition, some may continue to pray the entire time even as the group prays)
- ○ Scripture reading
- ○ Small-group prayer (1 minute per person)
- ○ After 3–5 minutes of prayer in groups, the leader prays a corporate prayer of confession
- ○ Song/hymn

---

1 Repeat for each section.

Section 2: Confession and repentance

Section 3: Thanksgiving

Section 4: Supplication

Section 5: Intercession (for community, nation, those outside the church)

Closing

- I like to end on a high note. Some prefer to end in lament.

- Prayer leader asks people to gather in a circle, signifying unity and prayer agreement.

- Leader asks three church leaders to pray in celebration, declaration, and blessing over the people present.

- Song of celebration and declaration.

- Closing testimonies and sending prayer.

Profile of Leaders Interviewed for This Book

The names of the pastors I interviewed have been changed, allowing them to speak candidly and to share stories without the risk of breaching trust.

Name: Pastor Charles
Role: Youth pastor
Denominational affiliation/tradition: None/African American
Generation: Millennial
Theological training: None/pastor's kid
Location: Southeast
Church size: 600

Name: Pastor Alex
Role: Youth pastor

Denominational affiliation/tradition: None/megachurch
Generation: Millennial
Theological training: Bible college
Location: Southwest
Church size: 1,200

Name: Pastor Misha
Role: Senior pastor
Denominational affiliation/tradition: Mennonite/Anabaptist
Generation: Millennial
Theological training: Bible college
Location: Southwest
Church size: 70

Name: Pastor Enrique
Role: Senior pastor
Denominational affiliation/tradition: Mennonite/
Anabaptist-evangelical
Generation: Millennial
Theological training: None/pastor's kid
Location: Midwest
Church size: 1,400

Name: Minister Chuck
Role: Church planter
Denominational affiliation/tradition: African American/para-
church ministries
Generation: Generation X
Theological training: Bible college/parachurch training
Location: Southwest
Church size: n/a

Notes

Introduction

1   Josh Packard and Ashleigh Hope, "The Dechurched as Religious Refugees," in *Church Refugees: Sociologists Reveal Why People Are Done with Church but Not Their Faith* (Loveland, CO: Group Publishing, 2015), 16.
2   "In U.S., Decline of Christianity Continues at Rapid Pace," Pew Forum, October 17, 2019, https://www.pewforum.org/2019/10/17/in-u-s-decline-of-christianity-continues-at-rapid-pace/.
3   Michael O. Emerson and Christian Smith, "The Organization of Religion," in *Divided by Faith: Evangelical Religion and the Problem of Race in America* (New York: Oxford University Press, 2000), 150–51.
4   Conrad L. Kanagy, "The Call," in *Road Signs for the Journey: A Profile of Mennonite Church USA* (Scottdale, PA: Herald Press, 2007), 73.
5   Kanagy, "God's People Now," in *Road Signs*, 52–53.

Chapter 1

1   Andrew E. Hill, "Ezra–Nehemiah," in *A Survey of the Old Testament*, by Andrew E. Hill and John H. Walton (Grand Rapids: Zondervan, 2000), 276.

2 Thom S. Rainer and Eric Geiger, "The Simple Revolution Has Begun," in *Simple Church: Returning to God's Process for Making Disciples* (Nashville: B & H Publishing Group, 2011), 14.

Chapter 2

1 *Becoming Five Multiplication Study Research Report* (Nashville: LifeWay Research, 2019), available at http://lifewayresearch.com/wp-content/uploads/2019/03/2019ExponentialReport.pdf.
2 http://lifewayresearch.com/wp-content/uploads/2019/03/2019ExponentialReport.pdf
3 Mark Chaves, Shawna Anderson, and Jason Byassee, *American Congregations at the Beginning of the 21st Century: A Report from the National Congregations Study* (Durham: Duke University, 2008), 2, available at https://sites.duke.edu/ncsweb/files/2019/03/NCSII_report_final.pdf
4 Matt Branaugh, "Willow Creek's 'Huge Shift,'" *Christianity Today*, May 15, 2008, http://www.christianitytoday.com/ct/2008/june/5.13.html.
5 Justin Champion, "Gutenberg's Bible: The Real Information Revolution," *History Today*, October 10, 2018, http://www.historytoday.com/reviews/gutenberg%E2%80%99s-Bible-real-information-revolution.

Chapter 3

1 Michael O. Emerson and Christian Smith, "From Separate Pews to Separate Churches," in *Divided by Faith: Evangelical Religion and the Problem of Race in America* (New York: Oxford University Press, 2000), 23.
2 Thom S. Rainer and Eric Geiger, *Simple Church: Returning to God's Process for Making Disciples* (Nashville: B&H Publishing Group, 2011), 111.
3 Harmeet Kaur, "A Church Made Headlines for Allegedly Asking Older Members to Leave. But the Reality Is More Complicated," CNN, January 22, 2020, http:// www.cnn.com/2020/01/22/us/grove-united-methodist-church-replanting-trnd/index.html.
4 Rainer and Geiger, *Simple Church*, 199.
5 Richard Koch, "Simple Is Beautiful," in *The 80/20 Principle: The Secret of Achieving More with Less* (New York: Currency, 2018), 88.

6 "Choosing a New Church or House of Worship," Pew Research Center, August 23, 2016, https://www.pewforum.org/2016/08/23/choosing-a-new-church-or-house-of-worship/.

Chapter 4

1 Mitchell Krucoff and Dianne Gallup, "Results of First Multi-center Trial of Intercessory Prayer, Healing Touch in Heart Patients," Duke Health, updated January 20, 2016, http://corporate.duke-health.org/news-listing/results-first-multicenter-trial-intercessory-prayer-healing-touch-heart-patients.

2 James Porter Moreland and Dallas Willard, "Why the Mind Matters in Christianity," in *Love Your God with All Your Mind: The Role of Reason in the Life of the Soul* (Colorado Springs: NavPress, 1997), 75.

3 J. Oswald Sanders, "Prayer and Leadership," in *Spiritual Leadership: Principles of Excellence for Every Believer* (Chicago: Moody Press, 1994), 88–89.

Chapter 5

1 J. Oswald Sanders, "Prayer and Leadership," in *Spiritual Leadership: Principles of Excellence for Every Believer* (Chicago: Moody Press, 1994), 28.

Chapter 6

1 The list below does not have the *inter-* prefix. Let me clarify, so I don't suffer that wrath of my fellow diversity, equity, and inclusion professionals. There are a few schools of thought about the inter-changeability of prefixes related to "cultural." Depending on what you are reading, you may come across the prefixes *inter-*, *intra-*, and *cross-*. They all have slightly different meanings that I do not believe change the core objective of diversity and inclusion work, that of being able to work across cultural differences effectively. In general, *inter-culturally* involves interactions among people from different cultures; *intra-culturally* involves the cultural differences within an identity group; *culturally* involves understanding the dominant culture; and *cross-culturally* involves a comparison of interactions among people from the same culture with those of people from another

culture. For our discussion, my focus is on intercultural interactions and the competencies necessary to facilitate those interactions.

2   Tim Brownlee and Kien Lee, "Section 7: Building Culturally Competent Organizations" in "Chapter 27: Cultural Competence in a Multicultural World" in *Community Tool Box*, Center for Community Health and Development, accessed December 5, 2020, http://ctb.ku.edu/en/table-of-contents/culture/cultural-competence/culturally-competent-organizations/main.

3   Daniel Hill and Brenda Salter McNeil, "Disorientation," in *White Awake: An Honest Look at What It Means to Be White* (Downers Grove, IL: InterVarsity Press, 2017), 93.

4   Katerina Bezrukova, Chester S. Spell, Jaime L. Perry, and Karen A. Jehn, "A Meta-Analytical Integration of Over 40 Years of Research on Diversity Training Evaluation," *Psychological Bulletin 142*, no. 11 (June 2014): 1227–74, https://doi.org/10.1037/bul0000067.

5   Linda-Eling Lee, Ric Marshall, Damion Rallis, and Matt Moscardi, *Women on Boards: Global Trends in Gender Diversity on Corporate Boards* (New York: MSCI ESG Research, 2015), 2.

Chapter 7

1   Martin Luther King Jr., "Watts," in *The Autobiography of Martin Luther King, Jr.*, ed. Clayborne Carson (New York: Grand Central Publishing, 1998), 293.

2   André Gingerich Stoner, "What Is Holistic Witness?" Mennonite Church USA, February 13, 2014, https://www.mennoniteusa.org/menno-snapshots/what-is-holistic-witness-2/.

3   André Gingerich Stoner, February 17, 2014, reply to Berry Friesen on Stoner, "What Is Holistic Witness?"

Chapter 8

1   "Grants for Playground Equipment: Funding Opportunities," Play & Park Structures, accessed November 18, 2020, https://www.playandpark.com/funding/grant-opportunities.

2   Martin Luther King Jr., *Where Do We Go from Here: Chaos or Community?* (New York: Harper and Row, 1967).

3   Adi Jaffe, "7 Spiritual Elements Critical for Addiction Recovery," *Psychology Today*, May 4, 2018, https://www.psychologytoday.com/

us/blog/all-about-addiction/201805/7-spiritual-elements-critical
-addiction-recovery.

4   Victor E. Kappeler, "A Brief History of Slavery and the Origins
of American Policing," Police Studies Online, January 7, 2014,
https://plsonline.eku.edu/insidelook/brief-history-slavery-and
-origins-american-policing.

5   Exec. Order No. 13,831, 83 FR 20715 (2018), text available at
https://www.federalregister.gov/documents/2018/05/08/2018-09895/
establishment-of-a-white-house-faith-and-opportunity-initiative.

6   "Wholistic Approach," Christian Community Development
Association, May 5, 2020, http://ccda.org/about/philosophy/
wholistic-approach/.

7   Scott T. Fitzgerald and Ryan Spohn, "Pulpits and Platforms: The
Role of the Church in Determining Protest among Black Americans," *Social Forces* 84, no. 2 (December 2005): 1016, https://doi
.org/10.1353/sof.2006.0014. Internal citations omitted.

8   Jeff Diamant and Besheer Mohamed, "Black Millennials Are
More Religious Than Other Millennials," Pew Research Center,
July 20, 2018, http://www.pewresearch.org/fact-tank/2018/07/20/
black-millennials-are-more-religious-than-other-millennials/.

Chapter 9

1   Dave Briggs, "What I Wish I Had Known about Stewardship,"
CT Pastors, November 13, 2018, http://www.christianitytoday.com/
pastors/2016/august-web-exclusives/what-i-wish-i-had-known
-about-stewardship.html.

2   Elaine Howard Ecklund and Deidra Carroll Coleman, "It's Hard
to Close Black Churches amid COVID-19," *Christianity Today*,
March 24, 2020, http://www.christianitytoday.com/ct/2020/march
-web-only/coronavirus-hard-to-close-black-churches-amid-covid-19
.html.

3   "Houston, we have a problem" is a misquotation from the
radio conversation between the astronaut John Swigert and the
NASA Mission Control Center in Houston during the Apollo 13
mission after the astronauts identified that an explosion had dam-
aged their spacecraft. (The original line was "Houston, we've had a
problem here.")

Resources

1 "GLAAD Media Reference Guide—Transgender," GLAAD, accessed February 5, 2020, https://www.glaad.org/reference/transgender.

2 K. Deaux and M. LaFrance, "Gender," in *The Handbook of Social Psychology* vol. 1, ed. Susan T. Fiske, Daniel T. Gilbert, and Gardner Lindzey (Boston: McGraw-Hill, 1998), 788–827.

3 "GLAAD Media Reference Guide—Transgender."

4 Dana S. Dunn and Shane Burcaw, "Thinking about Disability Identity: Major Themes of Disability Identity Are Explored," American Psychological Association, November 2013, http://www.apa.org/pi/disability/resources/publications/newsletter/2013/11/disability-identity.

5 *Merriam-Webster*, s.v. "nationality (*n.*)," accessed December 5, 2020, https://www.merriam-webster.com/dictionary/nationality.

6 See https://www.purdueglobal.edu/education-partnerships/generational-workforce-differences-infographic/

The Author

GLEN GUYTON is executive director of Mennonite Church USA, the first African American to serve in that role, and consults with leaders to help them reap the benefits of developing more diverse, inclusive, and culturally competent organizations. A proven leader, Guyton is a former Air Force officer and has years of experience serving in executive roles, coaching leaders, and cultivating relationships with diverse volunteers and donors. A father of two and a native of Houston, Texas, Guyton stays in shape and helps offset his passion for great food by running. He holds a BS in management from the U.S. Air Force Academy and an MS in education from Regent University. You can learn more about his work at GlenGuyton.com.